earringology

earringology

How to Make Dangles, Drops, Chandeliers & More

candie cooper

LARK JEWELRY
& BEADING

EDITORS
Nathalie Mornu
Kevin Kopp

ART DIRECTOR
Kathleen Holmes

BOOK & COVER DESIGN
Kay Holmes Stafford

PROJECT PHOTOGRAPHY
Lynne Harty

HOW-TO PHOTOGRAPHY
Candie Cooper

SKETCH ILLUSTRATIONS
Candie Cooper

ILLUSTRATION (PAGE 44)
Melissa Grakowsky Shippee

LARK JEWELRY & BEADING
An Imprint of Sterling Publishing
387 Park Avenue South
New York, NY 10016

© 2014 by Candie Cooper
Illustrations and how-to photography, and photos pages 10–19 © 2014 by Candie Cooper
All other photography © 2014 by Lark Books,
an Imprint of Sterling Publishing, Co., Inc.

ISBN 978-1-4547-0818-6

Library of Congress Cataloging-in-Publication Data

Cooper, Candie, 1979-
  Earringology : how to make dangles, drops, chandeliers & more / Candie Cooper.
    pages cm
  Includes index.
  ISBN 978-1-4547-0818-6
  1. Beadwork. 2. Earrings. 3. Jewelry making.
  I. Title. II. Title: How to make dangles, drops, chandeliers & more.
  TT860.C66268 2014
  745.594'2--dc23

            2013037666

Distributed in Canada by Sterling Publishing
c/o Canadian Manda Group, 165 Dufferin Street
Toronto, Ontario, Canada M6K 3H6
Distributed in the United Kingdom by GMC Distribution Services
Castle Place, 166 High Street, Lewes, East Sussex, England BN7 1XU
Distributed in Australia by Capricorn Link (Australia) Pty. Ltd.
P.O. Box 704, Windsor, NSW 2756, Australia

For information about custom editions, special sales, and premium and corporate purchases,
please contact Sterling Special Sales at 800-805-5489 or specialsales@sterlingpublishing.com.

Email academic@larkbooks.com for information about desk and examination copies.
The complete policy can be found at larkcrafts.com.

Every effort has been made to ensure that all the information in this book is accurate.
However, due to differing conditions, tools, and individual skills, the publisher cannot be
responsible for any injuries, losses, and other damages that may result
from the use of the information in this book.

Manufactured in China

2 4 6 8 10 9 7 5 3 1

larkcrafts.com
candiecooper.com

dedication

I'm dedicating this book to my husband, Aaron McCoart. We got married while this book was right in the middle of being written. Thank you for your constant support and enthusiasm about my work. I can keep moving forward towards my ideas, projects, and dreams because you help me to fly. You are my love.

a note from Candie

Photo by Nicole A. Howard

Hello fellow jewelry makers. My name is Candie Cooper and I am a jewelry designer with a passion for bold colors and a desire to twist and turn materials until they dance. I'm inspired by so many things, but most of all, I want my jewelry to tell a story: to describe a place I want to visit, bring back a nostalgic memory from childhood, to experience romance, and more...it's all in my jewelry.

Earringology is my fourth solo book with Lark Books. In the past ten years, I've authored *Necklaceology* (2012), *Metalworking 101 for Beaders* (2009), and *Felted Jewelry* (2007). I've also appeared on the PBS series, "Beads, Baubles, and Jewels." I love sharing my love of unique jewelry techniques with readers and viewers alike. Currently, I'm working on product development for the jewelry finding industry, cooking up new book ideas, and working with many craft companies to design new projects. I'm also teaching workshops at my hometown art center. Come visit my website and blog at candiecooper.com, and friend me on your favorite social networking sites so we can keep in touch.

contents

playful

The fun thing about making jewelry is you can create just about ANYTHING! So let's start here. From pink bells to little birds to letter tiles, you'll find all kinds of fun in this section.

laid back

I wear earrings when I walk my dog, while I'm at work, and to my nephew's birthday parties. Keep it simple with these straightforward yet stylish pairs.

bohemian

Let your free spirit shine with this stylish group. Dye, knot, paint, and wrap to your heart's content while making these earrings with a flair.

be bold

Don't get lost in the shuffle when it comes to accessorizing. Instead, make a statement with these bright and brash pieces.

chic

Look glamorous when you put a little sparkle and shine together in your creations. You'll be stylish day or night with these designer-looking earrings!

materials & tools

If you went to the flea market with me, you'd see that I like to pick through boxes of junk—I mean, ahem, treasures—to salvage vintage crystals and tiny toys for use in my jewelry. Yet, just as much as I like to repurpose, I also love to shop the DIY jewelry section of craft stores, as well as online independent retailers. So rest assured that you'll be able to find most of the materials described in this book from your usual sources. It is my hope that these projects will inspire you to design your own versions with readilibly available materials and the things you already have in your stash. Have fun and know I'm with you in spirit on those treasure hunts!

❶

bead types ❶

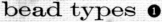

My head goes in ten different directions when I think about the word beads. Seasoned jewelry makers know that each bead has its place in a design. That's my excuse for having so many (hear me giggling) ziplock bags filled with beads, which is how I organize my bead stash. I have bags for round, rough cut, polished, pressed, faceted, half-drilled, spacers...I could go on and on when talking about beads.

Following are a few notes about the different kinds of beads you'll find in the earring projects described in this book. If you want to change the look of a design, simply start by using different the beads. For example, if a project uses crystals and you want an earthier look, replace the crystals with some gemstones or wood beads. Play around with the design and substiture your favorite beads until you get the look you want.

seed and bugle beads

Seed beads come in a variety of sizes indicated with an "aught" symbol: 1°, 4°, 6° and so on. The smaller the number, the bigger the bead. I categorize bugle beads here because they are also small, though tubular in shape. Seed beads can be perfectly smooth and uniform, others not so much.

gemstones

Gemstones are truly one of nature's beautiful treasures, coming in different cuts, colors, and qualities that determine their cost. You may notice a grade next to the name, like AA or B. The grading system tells a gem's desirability based on qualities such as clarity and color. At the end of the day, you need to examine what you are buying and make sure you're getting a fair price. I started out buying less expensive stones, but these days I'll spend extra to get what I consider a stunning strand.

crystals

My name is Candie, and I'm a sparkle addict. I think crystals are so pretty, but for a long time I thought I could only put them with other crystals. Recently, however, I've begun to place one here or one there in most of my designs. If you want to make a statement, put some crystals in your earrings—it's that easy! Bicones, rounds, helixes (twists), briolettes, and rondelles are just some of the faceted cuts you can use, and each one is sure to sparkle. An AB next to the crystal name means the gemstone has an iridescent-like, Aurora Borealis coating. You can never go wrong adding a little sparkle to your earrings.

Each bead is further decorated with glazes to add color and design elements. You can make your own ceramic beads as well as buy them.

resin or acrylic

Resin and acrylic beads are both made of a translucent, matte plastic material. Light passing through the frosted surface makes these beads look yummy. And, because acrylic is a synthetic formulation, you'll have boundless color options, too.

felt

I started out making my own felt beads, but now I buy them. If the bead is too big, try wetting it with soap and water and rolling it between your palms to make it smaller. Or you can make your own with sheets of felt.

wood

For an earthy feel, check out the wide variety of wood beads. You can purchase them stained in many colors or buy them unfinished if you want to paint and decorate them yourself. Some manufacturers are making decorative wood beads with patterns printed on them in bright colors.

czech glass

Shiny, fire-polished cathedral cuts and drakes are some of the shapes you'll find for Czech beads. You'll also find some that have been molded into shapes such as bugs, leaves, and butterflies, among others. In addition, the colors of Czech glass are amazing and vibrant.

pearl or freshwater beads

Pearls can be manufactured by man or made by nature. Their colors are radiant and their shapes can be perfectly round (you can find unique shapes as well). Freshwater pearls come in a wide variety of shapes, colors, and sizes. I love them for their organic, satin look.

shells

If you like beads that can illuminate elements of the design, look for shells. Some have been carved into shapes, perhaps dyed, or they may be left as found in nature. In any case, they are beautiful and cost effective to use in your jewelry.

ceramic

Ceramic beads are made from clay that may be molded or hand-formed and then fired in a kiln to make them sturdy.

decorative metal beads, spacer beads, and bead caps ❷

metal beads

Metal beads are always good things to have in your bead stash. Look for hollow, cast-metal beads to use when making earrings because the weight of some metal beads can feel cumbersome or even stretch your earlobes.

metal spacer beads

I have no shortage of tiny metal spacer beads: daisy spacers, plain spacers, brass, copper, silver, or others. I use them in 99 percent of my designs because they tie everything together and look great against a variety of materials.

bead caps

A bead cap is similar to a mat around a picture—it frames and showcases the bead. Cones, petals, and filigree are some of the variations of bead caps that I often use.

findings

Get familiar with words like ear wires, jump rings, head pins, eye pins, and crimp beads—the list could go on. Collectively, these are known as findings, and they come in a variety of metals and finishes, including base metal, silver plated, sterling, brass, pewter, gunmetal, brushed, antiqued (or oxidized), and others. Choosing findings isn't unlike choosing beads. For quick and fun costume-jewelry looks, use ones made of base metals. Designs that use precious-metal findings will cost more but also have a more expensive look. It's up to you.

If it's an option, try on different ear wire styles, to see if you like the design and the way they feel against your ear lobe. You can buy basic and plain commercial findings, but there are so many others that have added design elements, such as a crystal or a coil-wrapped embellishment.

ear wires and such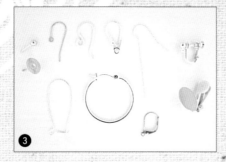

Almost all ear wires have a loop of some sort on which to add beaded dangles and charms. There are a number of different types of ear wires that are often used for making earrings.

French: French ear wires consist of a single, continuous wire. There is a loop at one end, and the wire continues to arch into a hook shape. They come in all sorts of metals and finishes. For a burst of color, check out niobium wires that can be found in yellow, green, aqua, blue, purple, and fuchsia. Niobium is considered hypoallergenic, by the way.

Kidney: Kidney ear wires are also made from one continuous arched wire that passes through the earlobe. It has a hook on one end so it latches to itself, making it secure.

Lever Back: Lever back ear wires have a hinged back piece that opens and closes, hence their name. This type of wire produces a very secure fit.

Post: Usually our pierced ear journey begins with post-style earrings. Jewelry makers can find decorative posts with loops that hold beaded dangles or chains.

Pad and Post: Some post earrings have a smooth pad where you may find a decorative element that allows you to attach an embellishment such as a button or flatback gem to it with cement.

Hoop: Earring hoops can have a variety of closures. A latch-back closure is one of the most common. Other hoops have hook or tubing closures to make the hoop one continuous circle.

Clip-on: Clip-on findings are for folks without pierced ears. These findings attach to earlobes with a hinged clip (that sometimes feels excruciating because it pinches your ear!). For a more comfortable fit, look for the type of adjustable clip-on findings that have a screw back, so that you can control how much pressure you add to your ear.

Handmade: You can make your own ear wires with sterling, silver-plated, or gold-filled wire. I like to use 20-gauge, half-hard wire because the diameter feels just right and the wire holds its shape.

Novelty Ear Wires:
Of course there are the classic wire findings for earrings, and then there are novelty styles of ear wires as well. I've come across novelty wires that are embellished with dragonflies, filigree, and bezels.

earring backs

If you're like me, you've lost an earring (or twenty) over the years. Here are a few backing options to keep those gems from falling out.

Rubber Ear Wire Guards: These are great for French wires. They are usually transparent rubber, which means they are also hypoallergenic and camouflaged!

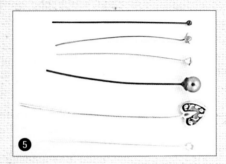

Butterfly Backs: This style of friction ear nut (that sounds like something you'd find in a hardware store, right?) is used with a post-style finding. It's called butterfly because of its shape. These are commonly used for petite, stud, or post-style earrings.

Comfort Grip with Barrel Back: This back piece is also for post earrings. It has a flat pad attached to it, to help balance and distribute the weight of the earring on the earlobe. The metal part of the barrel back is filled with rubber, so it grips the post in place, preventing it from sliding out.

additional types of findings

Head Pins and Eye Pins: ❺

Head pins are wires with a nail head or ball at one end. You can make beaded dangles by stringing beads onto them. This is what I used when I made my very first pair of earrings. These days, rather than a plain ball, head pins may also come with decorative "mounted ends," such as hearts, spirals, or crystals.

Eye pins are similar to head pins, except they have a loop on the end. They are typically used to make beaded links. You can buy eye pins or make your own with a short piece of wire. Just turn a simple loop at one end with your round-nose pliers, then reposition the pliers on the loop so you can center it over the straight part of the pin.

Rings: ❻

There are two different kinds of rings in this jewelry-making world—open and solid. Jump rings have been cut so you can open them up and use them to connect beaded elements and findings together. They come in different metals, thicknesses, and shapes, so you will find round, square, and oval jump rings. Solid jump rings also come in varied shapes, but with no opening. Solid rings are extra secure because other findings cannot sneak through the opening and fall off.

Fold-Over Findings, Chain Connectors, Pinch Bails: ❼

These days you can make jewelry from anything, but nontraditional materials sometimes need special types of findings. As usual, you'll have choices in sizes, metals, and finishes.

Fold-over findings are used to make secure connections or to finish the ends of leather, lace, ribbon, and more. The raw or cut end is glued into the open end of the finding, which often has some kind of connector at the other end, so you can attach a jump ring, link, or loop of some kind.

You'll need a special connector to link a crystal cup chain (it's called a pronged cup chain connector) or a ball chain (the ball chain connector with a loop) to your designs. It's been my experience that either of these can be readily found in independent bead stores.

A pinch bail isn't only for hanging a pendant on a chain. Use it to hang tiny crystal or gemstone drops from ear wires, too.

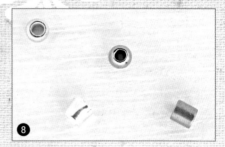

Filigree and Charms: ⑨

If you love vintage-looking jewelry, filigree pieces will make your heart flutter. They come in different shapes, from leaves to flowers to round or square. Their openings are great for hanging or stitching beads.

As for charms, they aren't just for bracelets! In your quest for making jewelry, you'll see teeny-tiny ones that can dangle from earrings as well!

Links: ⑩

I consider any finding to be a connector or link if it has holes on opposite ends. You can make earrings very easily with components like these. Connect one end to an ear wire and the opposite end to a beaded dangle. Earring finished! You may also find linking-type components made with lots of loops. These are chandelier findings. You can hang tons of beaded dangles and chains from them to create flashy earrings that have lots of movement.

strands, pigments, and sealers

beading wire and nylon filaments ⑪

Nylon-coated beading wire comes in many forms: silver-plated, brightly colored, and basic gray are a few of them. The thing to watch when making earrings—assuming that they will be lightweight—is the diameter of the wire being used. The wire's package indicates the single-strand diameter as well as the number of strands that make up the wire. Basically, the higher the strand count, the more flexible the wire will be, and larger diameters translate into stronger wires.

Nylon monofilament is a clear, non-fraying stringing material that is used for beadweaving (like the technique used in Atomium, page 43). You can also create illusion jewelry designs with it. I use the polyfilament style to hold seed beads and for weaving and knotting techniques. It has a silky look to it, but is actually a polyester material that keeps its smooth finish and holds knots tight.

Crimp Beads and Tubes: ⑧

Crimp beads and tubes are similar, with the main difference being that crimp beads have seams and tubes do not. If you've ever done crimping with strung pieces, you may have had a round crimp bead crack at the seam. For me, this causes crimping anxiety, so I've switched to tubes for the most part.

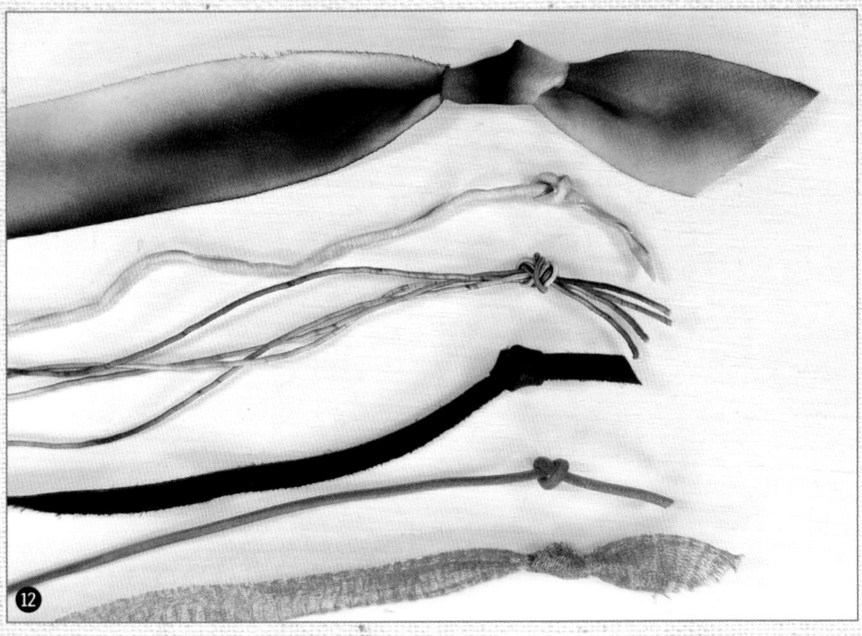

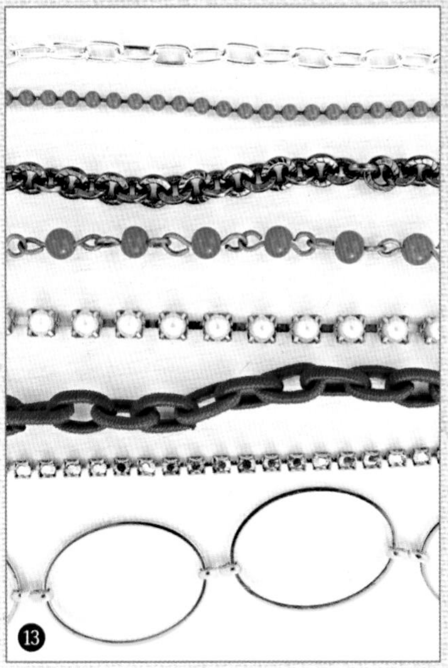

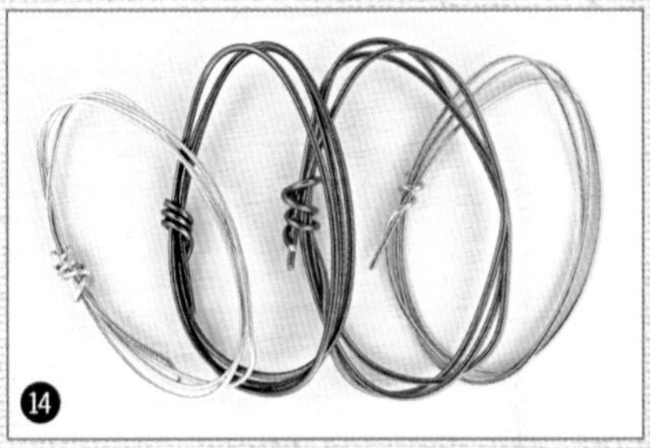

leather cord, ribbon, wire mesh ⓬

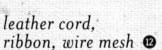

I love leather, and now craft stores are adding more and more variations. Leather cords are available in the softer Greek style, a more rigid Indian type, as well as the suede-lace variety. You can even find it with metallic finishes that lend a wonderful bohemian-looking sparkle.

Ribbons are a way to add a Victorian or vintage appeal to designs. And don't forget to look for hand-dyed dupioni silk and lace pieces. Wire mesh is a delicate, lacy ribbon that is actually made of fine metal wire. It comes in a variety of colors. You can stretch it, shape it, or leave it flat; the possibilities are endless. It's also sold in a mesh tube style.

chain ⓭

Now that I think about it, I love chain as much as leather. There are so many beautiful and unique chains. Colorful ball chain, pearl chain, crystal chain, gunmetal, shiny silver, and large links can all really set your designs apart. Even large-link chain can be broken apart to make it useable in earrings. But remember to keep in mind how much the chain weighs when considering it for an earring project.

wire ⓮

Wire comes in all kinds of metal materials, sizes, and shapes, so its use will depend on the project you are making. Craft wire may be color-coated, or made of copper, brass, or sterling silver (which is hypoallergenic), and comes in twisted, half-round, or square shapes. The diameter of wire is indicated in gauges. In all cases, the smaller the gauge number, the thicker the wire. If you plan to make your own ear wires, you'll need 20-gauge, half-hard sterling silver wire.

pigments

You can easily customize commercial findings by adding a dash of color. There are a few options for doing this. First, you can use special multipurpose acrylic paints or opaque inks on metal, glass, or ceramic. Brush on some strokes or apply dots with the end of a paintbrush. Secondly, you can find transparent alcohol inks that can tint metal, fibers, or glass by applying them with felt squares. These look especially great on embossed pieces.

sealers

There are lots of pieces in this book with custom surfaces. Protect those precious layers with different glazes and sealers. For the multipurpose acrylic paints or opaque inks, use a specially formulated glaze that goes on with a brush. You can leave a

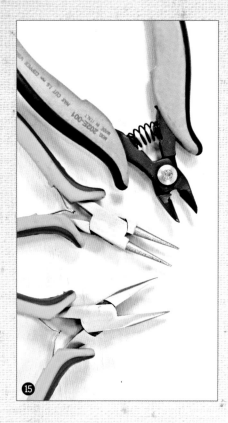

wire cutters

I give my wire cutters a hard workout when I'm making earrings. You'll reach for them over and over to snip wire, nylon filament, cord, and the like.

round-nose pliers

The conical-shaped jaws of these pliers are especially useful in forming a loop at the end of a wire.

chain-nose pliers

At a glance, chain-nose pliers look like round-nose pliers because they both have tapered noses. Take a closer look and you will see that the chain-nose jaws are flat on the inside. This makes them good for opening and closing jump rings and getting into snug spaces.

bead board and mat

A bead board may seem like overkill, especially for making tiny earrings, but I still find the board's ridges useful for lining up beads to see how they look next to each other. I also keep a stack of bead mats next to my worktable. If you've had a bead (or 70!) roll off your table, get a bead mat. They are awesome for this type of work.

jig 16

A jig is a block with grid-patterned holes in it. The holes hold perfectly fitted pegs. Jigs are great for forming ear wires because the pegs keep the shape consistent. You will find several versions of jigs for making jewelry. Often you can purchase a jig in the jewelry-making section of your local craft store, or make your own with a wood block and dowel rods.

chasing hammer and steel bench block 17

A chasing hammer is specially made for jewelry making. Compare the face of a carpenter's hammer to a chasing hammer and you'll see that the jeweler's tool is super shiny instead of dull and dented. This is significant if you plan on making your own ear wires, because you can add strength to ear wires by hammering them on a polished and tempered steel bench block with a chasing hammer, as seen in Twirled (page 48).

cutting and smoothing

Cup Burr: A cup burr is a special cutting tool that rounds and smoothens the ends of wires so they aren't sharp. You can buy the kind that you turn by hand or one that attaches to a multipurpose rotary tool.

decoupaged surface alone because it acts as a sealer once it's dry. However, for many treated surfaces, I like to use an acrylic sealer. Most often I use a brush-on formula, but if your surface is delicate, use a spray varnish instead.

basic tools 15

There are at least three tools that no jewelry maker can do without. They are: wire cutters, round-nose pliers, and chain-nose pliers. The price for pliers can vary depending on their quality. If you're planning on making a lot of jewelry, I suggest investing in a good set of these basic types.

Bead Reamer, File, Abrasive Block, and Polishing Cloth: ⑱
Sometimes the holes in beads aren't big enough (especially in pearls). You'll need a bead reamer to widen the holes. Try a #2 hand file to smooth and round off wire ends. Use a sanding block with multiple grits on each side or an emery board to remove a patina or to add texture to smooth metal surfaces. Try a special jewelry polishing cloth to remove oxidation from sterling ear wires, making them clean and shiny. You can usually pick up these items in the jewelry sections of craft stores.

drilling and punching holes ⑲

I've simplified the hole-making process for this book. For thin metal, try a hole punch made for metal. For wood or acrylic, I suggest a twist drill. This tool has a chuck at the end so it can hold tiny drill bits (numbers 55 and 60 are among the most useful for these projects).

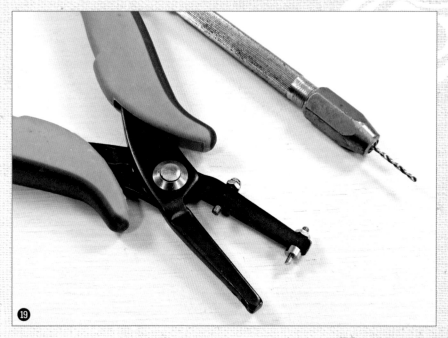

mandrels

To make the hook of an ear wire, you often need something circular around which you can wrap the end of the wire. You can keep it simple by using a dowel with a diameter of ¾ inch (2 cm), or you can buy a small bezel mandrel, which is tapered, so you can make various-sized hooks.

adhesives

Several different kinds of adhesives are useful for making earrings, as well as any other type of beaded jewelry.

Clear Jeweler's Cement: This is strong stuff for use when you want to rely on a long-lasting bind. Available through craft and beading stores, it comes in a tube with a precision tip so you can control exactly where to place it for detail work, and will dry clear. Always take care to work in a ventilated area when using this or any other kind of glue.

White Glue: For times when the extra-strength jeweler's cement is not necessary, it might be handy to have this type of tacky, thick craft glue available.

miscellaneous items ⑳

Some miscellaneous tools you may be likely to need are scissors, a ruler or tape measure, permanent markers, jewelry shears, and double-sided tape. Be safe and make sure to wear glasses whenever drilling or cutting wires.

techniques

making ear wires

It's easy to make ear wires with a wire jig and your choice of 20-gauge wire. Use photo 1 as a guide for where to place the pegs in the jig. To start, make a small loop at the end of a piece of wire with the tips of the round-nose pliers. Since this is where beaded dangles will connect, the loop doesn't have to be very large. Arrange seven pegs in a jewelry jig as shown. Slide the loop over the starting peg. Lead the wire up, around, and down, as shown. Snip the wire end to the desired length and voilà! One wire is finished! You can tweak the shape of the ear wire with chain-nose pliers at this point to get it looking exactly the way you want.

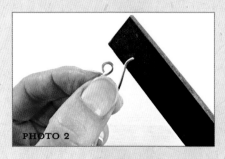

PHOTO 2

PHOTO 3

PHOTO 4

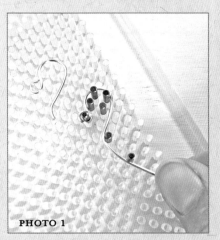

PHOTO 1

Smooth the sharp edges of the wire's ends with a file (photo 2). Use a sanding block to finish the edges (photo 3). Check the wire end with your thumb to make sure it can't scratch your earlobe.

Lastly, to make sure the ear wire remains rigid, hammer the front-facing part of it a few times on a steel block, using the flat side of a chasing hammer (photo 4). This process is called work hardening because it makes the wire stronger as you compact its metal

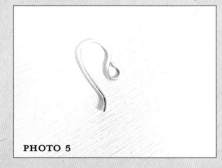

PHOTO 5

particles (photo 5). You can also texture other metal objects or ear wires by using the round end of the chasing hammer, or other texture tools.

connection findings

opening and closing loops and jump rings

You will need chain-nose pliers to open and close loops and jump rings. Don't open a finding by pulling its ends laterally apart from each other. It's important to open rings and loops of any kind by holding the finding firmly in one hand while grasping the wire next to the opening with your chain-nose pliers and twisting it toward you (photo 6). This will keep the loop or ring in its original shape. Close the piece using the same technique; just reverse the twisting direction.

PHOTO 6

making loops

Making a loop at the end of a head pin is the easiest way to make an earring— and, I might add, it's fast! Perfect loops take practice, but don't worry if you've never made one before. Just grab your basic pliers, beads, head pins, and wire cutters. Pop a cheesy romantic comedy into the DVD player and start practicing.

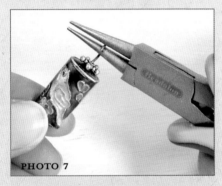

PHOTO 7

Simple Loop: To make a simple loop, start by stringing some beads or other dangle pieces onto a head pin. Using round-nose pliers, make a 90° bend at the end of the head pin and trim, leaving approximately ⅜ inch (1 cm) of space between the last element you strung and the bend in the wire. Use the round-nose pliers to roll the ex- tended portion of the head pin around so its end meets the rest of the pin next to the beads (photo 7). Adjust so the loop is completely closed.

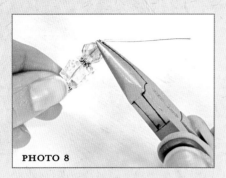

PHOTO 8

Wrapped Loop: Begin the process as if you were making a simple loop. Grasp the head pin above the last bead with chain-nose pliers and make a bend (photo 8). Now hold the wire with round-nose pliers and wrap the end of the wire up and around the top of the pliers and around the base of the wire (photo 9). Trim the excess wire from the coil. This technique creates a secure beaded dangle (photo 10).

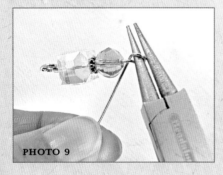

PHOTO 9

PHOTO 10

finishing the ends

chain connectors

I adore pearl and crystal chain. Thankfully these types of chain are easy to use in designs with special connectors that have prongs on them. Attach the connector to the end of the chain by rolling each of the connector's four prongs over the top of the pearl or crystal, using chain-nose pliers (photos 11, 12).

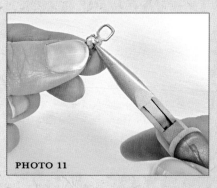

PHOTO 11

PHOTO 12

leather and ribbon connectors

Fold-over findings make it possible to attach leather and ribbon cords to jump rings and chain. Simply lay the cord in the finding, so that the connector's flaps are on either side. Use your trusty chain-nose pliers to fold over each flap (photo 13). Finish it with one big squeeze, to secure the finding to the cord.

PHOTO 13

crimping

We're going to keep it simple when it comes to crimping and only talk about a flat crimp, which means you use chain-nose pliers to literally flatten the crimp bead (or tube) into a square or rectangle. This simple method works with earrings for two reasons: firstly, earrings aren't as long or heavy as necklaces, which need proper crimping. Secondly, this style of crimping can be used to create the illusion that beads are suspended on a wire when they're actually held in place by the crimp beads.

making holes

There are a couple of ways to make holes in materials. The first is simple, using a special hole punch for metal. It works just like a regular paper hole punch, except it's strong so it cuts through thin metal. The punch is especially nice because you don't have to clean the burred edge that typically results from using a drill bit or a nail to make the hole.

PHOTO 14

Another way to make holes, especially when working with alternative materials such as wood and resin, is to use a manual twist drill (photo 14). Slow and steady is the motto for this technique. The drill bit itself sits in a chuck handpiece. All you have to do is mark where you want the hole with a permanent marker and then twist away. If you expect to be making lots of holes, you might instead opt for a multipurpose rotary tool. This versatile and powerful electrical tool accepts all kinds of accessory bits that can drill, polish, and smooth surfaces.

finishes

customizing surfaces with color

You're already creating custom jewelry, so why not create custom finishes within your designs? In addition to texture (see page 16), an easy way to alter surfaces is to add color to findings. There are a few ways to do this.

Liver of sulfur: I like texture on metal. Period. With textures, however, comes the question of how to emphasize their somewhat subtle look. One way is with liver of sulfur (LOS). It's smelly, but this tried-and-true mixture can oxidize silver, silver plate, and copper metal pieces. I used to buy LOS in rock form, but now I buy the simple-to-use gel formula. To use it, first clean the piece you wish to color with soap and water to remove residual oils. Follow the manufacturer's instructions

PHOTO 15

PHOTO 16

when mixing the LOS solution. I like to blend mine in a plastic container. Once mixed, the chemicals make a yellowish solution into which you can drop your metal component. After a suitable amount of time (again, check the directions!), use tweezers to pull the piece out of the LOS bath to check it (photo 15). Leave it in the solution until the desired color is reached. Use pumice and water to remove the oxidation from the raised portions of the metal (photo 16). Now you can either dry the piece or polish it with a brass brush and soapy water, to give it a shine.

PHOTO 17

Alcohol Inks and Patinas: Add color to metal, wood, shell, and more with alcohol inks and patinas (photo 17). Alcohol inks are transparent, whereas colored patinas are opaque. To use the alcohol ink, add a drop of it to a scrap of felt. Blot the colored patch of felt onto your piece (it dries fast!).

Other patinas can be applied with a brush. Mix the patina with a stirrer before brushing it on. Use a heat tool to speed up the drying time. Finally, scuff the surface of the piece with an abrasive block, to remove as much of the color from the surface of your piece as you like (see Dragonfly Tales, page 84, for an example of the final effect). Seal the treated surfaces with an acrylic varnish of your choice.

Enamel Paints: Enamels are also a great way to add dots of color to the surface of your design elements. Enamel paints are more durable than regular acrylic paints and usually need to be heat-set if you want to speed their longer curing time. Apply dots of enamel paint to metal with either the brush or the handle end of a paintbrush.

polishing

What do you do when earring wires and parts get tarnished? When I was in metalworking school, I was taught to use compounds and a fast-spinning muslin wheel to buff and polish the metal, so it would end up nice and shiny. Those were the good ol' days (though many manufacturers still use that technique). However, now I skip all that and use a yellow polishing cloth (photo 18). These cloths are impregnated with buffing compound. It removes the tarnish as you massage the jewelry component. The harder you work, the shinier your metal gets!

PHOTO 18

pink blossom bells

I love the simplicity of this design. These delicate resin flowers with silver accents can be worn to ring in spring and celebrate my ever growing obsession with cherry blossoms.

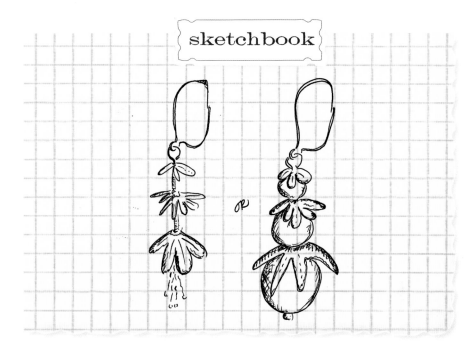

MATERIALS

2 pink Lucite flower beads, 5 x 13 mm

2 burgundy Lucite flower beads, 5 x 13 mm

2 pink Lucite flower beads, 7 x 12 mm

4 silver bugle beads, ¼ inch (0.6 cm) or 3°

2 silver spacer beads, 5 mm

6 silver balled head pins, 2 inches (5.1 cm) long

2 silver eye pins, 2 inches (5.1 cm) long

2 balled French ear wires

TOOLS

Wire cutters

Chain-nose pliers

Round-nose pliers

DIMENSIONS

½ x 1⅞ inches (1.3 x 4.8 cm)

procedure

1 For the dangles, make simple loops at the ends of three balled head pins. Trim any excess wire so that the finished length is ⅝ inches (photo 1).

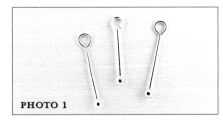

PHOTO 1

2 Open the loop on an eye pin with chain-nose pliers and connect the head-pin dangles (photo 2).

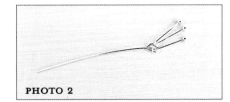

PHOTO 2

3 On the eye pin, string a large pink flower, a bugle bead, a burgundy flower, another bugle bead, a small pink flower, and a spacer bead (photo 3). Finish the end of the eye pin by making a simple loop.

PHOTO 3

4 Open the loop on one of the ear wires, and connect the flower piece to it (photo 4).

Repeat steps 1 through 4 to make the second earring.

PHOTO 4

MATERIALS

4 silver crimp beads

1 bag of flat, round sequins, ⅛ inch (0.3 cm) in diameter, assorted colors

2 silver jump rings, 5 mm

Satin-silver 7-strand beading wire, .015

2 French ear wires with geometric texture detail and solid loops

TOOLS

Chain-nose pliers

Wire cutters

DIMENSIONS

1⅞ inches x ⅞ inches (4.8 x 2.2 cm)

dancing

Sparkly and lightweight, strung sequins are so much fun. I feel like spinning on the dance floor whenever I wear a pair like this.

procedure

1 Cut two pieces of beading wire, each 4 inches (10.2 cm) long. String a length of sequins 3 inches (7.6 cm) long onto one of the wires (photo 1).

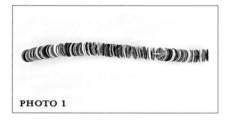

PHOTO 1

2 String a crimp bead onto the wire and thread the tail through the crimp bead, making a small loop. Use the chain-nose pliers to flatten the crimp bead (photo 2).

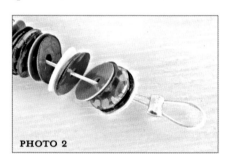

PHOTO 2

3 Add another crimp bead at the other end of the wire, compress it, flat crimp, and trim any excess wire (photo 3).

PHOTO 3

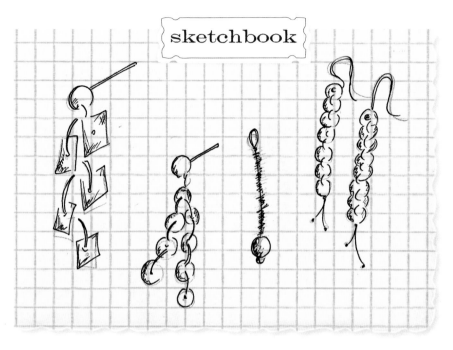

sketchbook

4 Open one of the jump rings with the chain-nose pliers. Connect both ends of the sequin strand and also a French ear wire to the jump ring; then close it (photo 4).

PHOTO 4

Repeat these steps to make the second earring.

VARIATION

up, up, and away

Who remembers that song from the 1960s by the Fifth Dimension (look it up if you don't)? Floating and dreaming without a care in the world, you'll have your head in the clouds when you put on this pair of earrings.

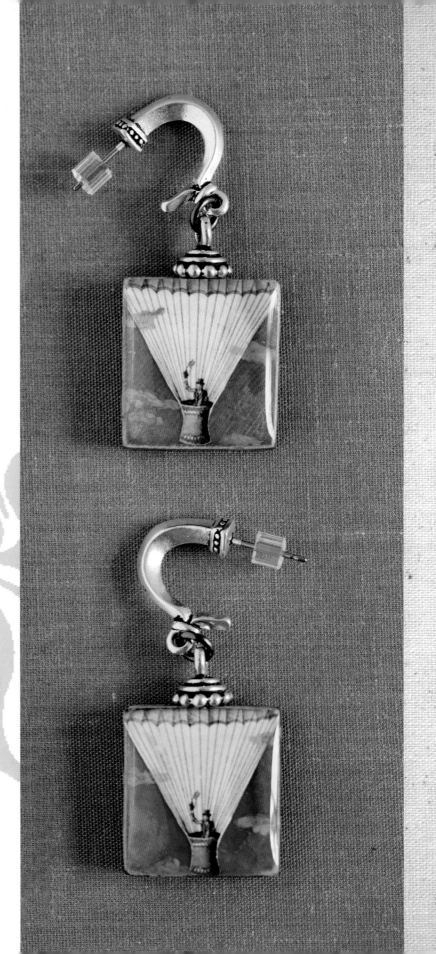

procedure

1 Stain the wood tiles by applying alcohol ink to a felt pad and rubbing it all over the tiles (photo 1).

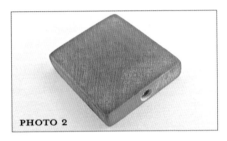

PHOTO 1

2 Drill a bead hole lengthwise through each of the tiles (photo 2).

PHOTO 2

3 Distress the edges of the tiles by removing some of the stain with sandpaper (photo 3).

PHOTO 3

4 Cut the images out of the collage sheet (photo 4). With the bead holes oriented at the top of the tiles, use the glue stick to attach an image to a face of each of the tiles.

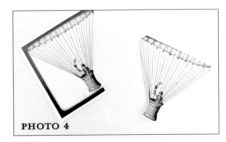

PHOTO 4

5 Use the paintbrush and acrylic paints to add details to the tiles (clouds, more balloon imagery), as shown in photo 5.

PHOTO 5

PHOTO 6

6 Use the jeweler's cement to set a bail finding into the bead holes, with the loop perpendicular to each of the tile faces, as shown in photo 7. Set it aside to dry.

PHOTO 7

7 Seal the images with an epoxy sticker (photo 6).

PHOTO 8

8 After the glue has dried, attach each of the painted-tile dangles to a hoop post with a gunmetal jump ring (photo 8).

I'll fly away

These butterflies are so light!
They make me want to flutter away
right along with them.

procedure

1 Punch out four butterfly shapes, two from each of the colored plastic sheets. As shown in photo 1, I chose pink and yellow.

PHOTO 1

2 Align two differently colored butterfly shapes, one behind the other. Use the ⅟₁₆-inch (1.6 mm) hole punch to make a hole in the top center of each, as shown in photo 2.

PHOTO 2

3 Put the un-flared end of an eyelet through both butterfly layers. Set the eyelet, flared side down, onto the steel block. Set the center punch into the eyelet and strike the end of the punch with a mallet, so that the walls of the eyelet tube roll neatly down (photo 3).

PHOTO 3

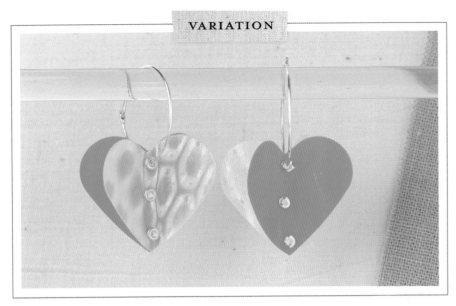

PHOTO 4

4 Repeat the process, using the hole punch to make a second hole below the first. Set the second eyelet, as described in step 3. To give the wings some dimension, bend the plastic wing pieces, as shown in photo 4.

PHOTO 5

5 Cut a piece of chain so it measures 1½ inches (3.8 cm), and attach a butterfly to the end of the chain with a 3-mm jump ring (photo 5).

6 Attach the other end of the chain to one of the ear wires with a 3-mm jump ring (photo 6).

PHOTO 6

NOTE:

You may need to remove an extra link or two of chain so that the butterfly hangs frontward.

Repeat steps 2 through 6 to make the second earring.

colored pencil

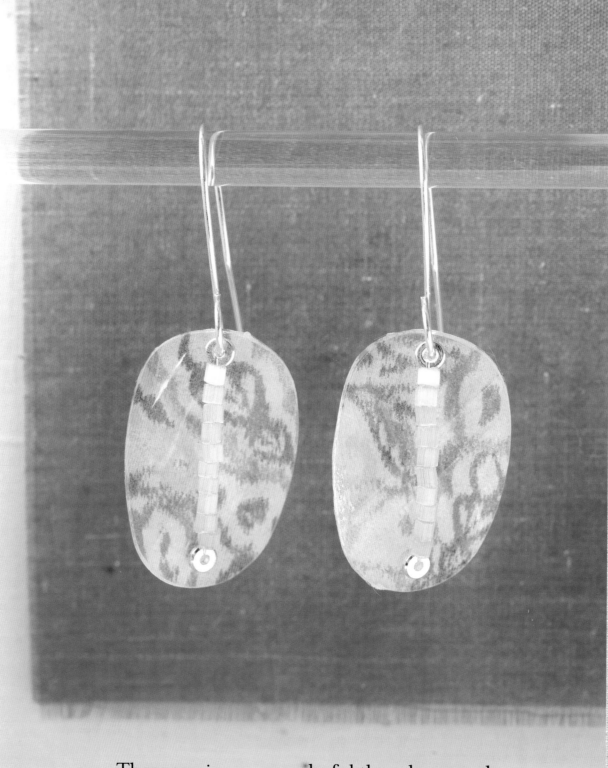

These earrings are so playful they almost make
me feel like a kid again. The pattern
on the washi tape reminds me of drawing with
colored pencils.

procedure

1 Cover one side of an acrylic link with a piece of the washi tape (photo 1). This will be the back side of the earring. Trim the excess with small scissors.

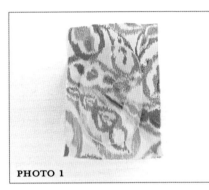

PHOTO 1

2 String a silver spacer bead, 10 seed beads, and another silver spacer onto the tail of the spool of nylon thread. Push the beads away from the thread end, so you can pass a section of un-beaded tail through the front of the acrylic link to the washi side. Cut the length of beaded thread off the spool, leaving another generous tail.

3 Tie the thread tails together on the washi side of the link and dot the knot with cement, to secure it there (photo 2). Closely trim both thread tails.The column of seed beads will fall down the front of the link, on the side opposite the washi tape.

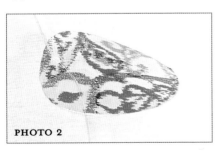

PHOTO 2

PHOTO 3

4 Open the loop on an ear wire. Pass the opened loop through the acrylic link and one of the silver spacer beads. Close the loop (photo 3).

Repeat steps 1 through 4 to make the second earring.

VARIATION

MATERIALS

2 faceted acrylic links, ¾ x 1 inches (1.9 x 2.5 cm)

4 silver spacer beads, 4 mm

20 green transparent 10° seed beads

2 large, looped French ear wires

Washi tape, 1 inch (2.5 cm) wide

Nylon thread

TOOLS

Chain-nose pliers

Small, sharp scissors

Clear, multipurpose jeweler's cement with a precision applicator tip

DIMENSIONS

2 x ⅞ inches (5.1 x 2.2 cm)

birds

Like the rest of the planet, I love birds.
Here's a playful pair I modeled from a
similar set a friend gave me as a gift. (Hers
were made entirely of real feathers and
perched on little brass bars.)
Sweet and inspiring.

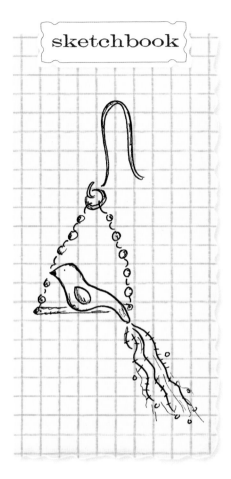

procedure

1 Roll some clay into two balls, each ½ inch (1.3 cm) in diameter. Pinch each ball into the shape of a bird. They don't have to be perfect (mine surely are not!). Use a toothpick to poke a hole in the ends of the tails, where you will add feathers, and in the heads, for each of the birds' eyes (photo 1).

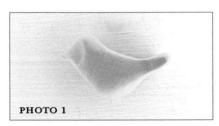

PHOTO 1

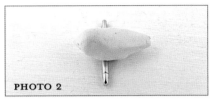

PHOTO 2

2 Set each bird on a brass bead bar; then add a little bit of clay, to secure the birds to the bars (photo 2).

3 Bake the birds according to the clay manufacturer's instructions. Paint the cured clay with watered-down acrylic paints. Sometimes I add two or three layers of paint, letting each layer dry between coats. Seal the pieces with a final coat of acrylic varnish (photo 3). Dab a smidge of gold paint on the beaks.

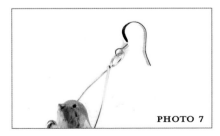

PHOTO 3

Optionally, you can cut wings from paper and glue them to the sides of the birds with a decoupage medium (photo 4). Seal the wings to the clay with the same decoupage medium.

PHOTO 4

4 Cut about 4 inches (10.2 cm) of wire. Wrap one end of the wire to the end of a bead bar. Do the same with the wire's free end at the other end of the bead bar. Make a twist or two at the top of the wire to create a loop (photo 5). Slide one jaw of the round-nose pliers into the loop to perfect the shape. This is the bird's perch.

PHOTO 5

5 Use the cement to attach a feather in the hole at the tail end of the clay bird (photo 6).

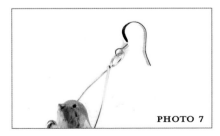

PHOTO 6

6 Open the ear wire's loop with the chain-nose pliers and attach it to the perch's loop you made in step 4 (photo 7).

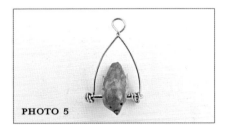

PHOTO 7

Repeat steps 4 through 6 to finish making the second earring.

beach stones

MATERIALS

2 pieces of similarly sized beach glass

4 green droplet beads, 6 x 4 mm

8 smooth silver spacer beads

2 cubic zirconia ear studs with loops

2 silver jump rings, 7 mm

16 silver jump rings, 5 mm

2 three-hole silver spacer bars, 18 x 6 mm

2 two-hole silver spacer bars, 8 x 4 mm

2 sections of rhodium curb chain, 1 inch (2.54 mm) each

Tinned copper wire, 24 gauge

Green alcohol ink

TOOLS

Wire cutters

Chain-nose pliers

Round-nose pliers

Multipurpose rotary tool with a 1.5-mm diamond drill bit

DIMENSIONS

3 x ½ inches (7.6 x 1.3 cm)

I collected this beach glass on the coast of Italy.
It was astonishing to see so much of it rolling in with
the tides. When I look at each piece, I wonder
where it came from—a wine bottle off a pirate ship?
Was there a message in the bottle?

procedure

1 Drill a hole near the edge of both the pieces of beach glass with the rotary tool, dipping the bit in water every few seconds (photo 1).

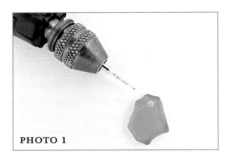
PHOTO 1

2 Wrap one of the beach stones with the wire in any pattern you like (photo 2). Twist the ends of wire on the back and trim away the excess.

PHOTO 2

3 Create the chain-and-link section. Use one of the larger jump rings (7 mm) to connect the beach stone to one of the three-hole spacer bars. Connect the opposite end of the link to one of the rhodium chain sections with one of the smaller jump rings. Use another small jump ring to connect the other end of the chain to a two-hole spacer bar (photo 3).

PHOTO 3

PHOTO 4

4 To make a dangle, create a wrap on a droplet bead by cutting a 3-inch (7.6 cm) section of wire and threading it through the bead's hole. Bring one side of the wire up (photo 4) while wrapping the opposite wire end around the top of the bead. When the hole in the bead is completely covered, trim the wire and tuck the end into the wrap. Finish the remaining side of the wire with a wrapped loop (photo 5). Trim any excess.

PHOTO 5

Repeat this step to make a second dangle for one of the earrings.

PHOTO 6

5 Use the 5-mm jump rings to connect the two green dangles and four of the silver spacer beads in a random pattern along the length of the chain-and-link portion you have made (photo 6).

6 Tint the cubic zirconia stones that are in each of the ear studs with green alcohol ink and lay them aside to dry (photo 7).

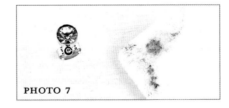
PHOTO 7

7 Connect one of the studs to the free end of the two-hole spacer bar with a small jump ring (photo 8).

PHOTO 8

Repeat steps 3 through 7 to complete the second earring.

MATERIALS

Twig, 1 inch (2.5 cm)
   long x 7/16 inch
   (11 mm) in diameter
2 brass head pins,
   2 inches (5.1 cm) long
2 brass domed bead
   caps, 6 mm
2 brass decorative bead
   caps, 6 mm
2 brass spacer beads,
   3 mm
2 textured brass jump
   rings, 8 mm
2 large kidney ear wires
Acrylic paint in brown,
   aqua, and orange
Acrylic varnish, gloss
   finish
Gold leaf

TOOLS

Wire cutters
Chain-nose pliers
Round-nose pliers
Small wood saw
Fine sandpaper
Multipurpose rotary
   tool and #55 drill bit
Paintbrush
Small flat plastic plate,
   for a palette
Toothpick

DIMENSIONS

2¾ inches (7 cm)

a walk in the woods

A walk in the woods has always been one of my favorite activities. One day about ten years ago I cut some twigs for beads and have had them in my stash ever since. This is a wonderful way to finally use a couple of them.

procedure

1 Use the saw to cut the twig in half (photo 1). Lightly sand the cut edges of both pieces to remove any rough spots.

PHOTO 1

2 Drill a center hole in each of the two twig pieces, using the rotary tool and bit (photo 2). Paint the cut surfaces of the twig pieces with aqua paint, and set them aside to dry on their sides.

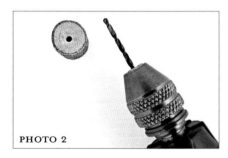

PHOTO 2

3 Put some acrylic varnish on the plate, and tint it with a drop of orange and a drop of brown paint.

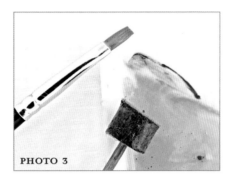

PHOTO 3

4 Slide one of the twig pieces onto a toothpick and seal it entirely with the tinted varnish (photo 3).

5 While the varnish is still tacky, drop pieces of gold leaf onto the bark surface (photo 4). Let the varnish dry; then seal the wooden twig-bead with three coats of varnish.

PHOTO 4

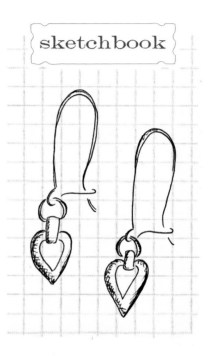

6 String a bead cap, the finished twig-bead, a decorative bead cap, and a brass spacer onto a head pin. Finish the end of the head pin with a wrapped loop. Use the wire cutters to trim the excess wire. Open a textured jump ring and use it to connect the kidney ear wire to the twig dangle.

Repeat steps 4 through 6 with the other twig piece to make the second earring.

change it up

The useful thing about this pair is that you can make additional layers, which means you can change them to suit your style on any particular day.

MATERIALS

2 teal rhinestones,
  4 mm
2 aluminum discs,
  ⅝ inch (1.6 cm) in
  diameter
2 aluminum flower
  posts with glue-in
  cups, 5 mm
Silver wire, 20 gauge
Alcohol ink in fuschia

TOOLS

Wire cutters
Round-nose pliers
Hand-held metal hole
  punch, 1-mm hole
  size
Dapping block and
  punch set
Plastic mallet
Chasing hammer
Steel block
Clear, multipurpose
  jeweler's cement
  with a precision
  applicator tip

DIMENSIONS

⅝ inch (1.6 cm) in
  diameter

procedure

1 Punch holes in the center of the discs (photo 1).

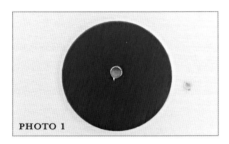

PHOTO 1

2 Set a disc into a recessed area on the dapping block. With the punch on top of the disc, strike the punch handle with a mallet. Continue the dapping until the disc is curved to your liking (photo 2). Repeat the process for the second disc.

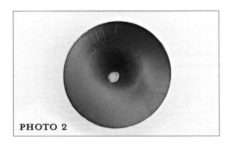

PHOTO 2

3 Use the round-nose pliers to make a silver-wire spiral that will fit inside one of the dapped discs. Flatten the spiral (photo 3) with a chasing hammer on a steel block.

PHOTO 3

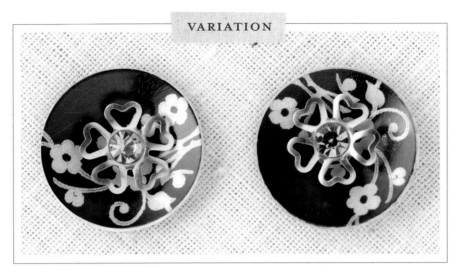

PHOTO 4

4 Coat a flower post with alcohol ink. After the color has dried, glue a rhinestone to the center of the flower (photo 4).

PHOTO 5

5 Apply a touch of cement to the back of the flower post and hold the center loop of the wire spiral to the glued spot until the cement dries (photo 5).

6 Nestle the flower-spiral into the recessed area of the disc (photo 6).

PHOTO 6

Repeat steps 3 through 6 to complete the second earring.

Decorate more flower posts and aluminum discs so you can change things up from time to time.

celebration

MATERIALS

8 blue matte glass
   beads, 5 x 1.5 mm
8 blue seed beads, 10°
8 brass textured spacer
   beads, 5 mm
2 oxidized brass lan-
   tern-shaped beads,
   5 mm
2 oxidized brass eye
   pins*
10 oxidized brass head
   pins, 24 gauge, 1 inch
   (2.5 cm) long
2 oxidized brass flower
   bead caps, 10 mm
2 oxidized brass flower
   bead caps, 6 mm
Oxidized brass chain,
   3-mm links
2 oxidized brass lever
   back ear wires
Red faux suede,
   4 inches (10.2 cm)
   square

* Or make your own
   from 1-inch (2.5 cm)
   pieces of 24-gauge
   wire.

TOOLS

Wire cutters
Chain-nose pliers
Round-nose pliers
Scissors
Fabric adhesive

DIMENSIONS

3¼ x ⁷⁄₁₆ inches
   (8.3 x 1.1 cm)

This pair of earrings was made on the 4th of July.
I had just gotten the red suede and was playing
around with it, wondering how I could use it in a
pair of earrings—here is the result.

procedure

1 Cut a circle of faux suede 3½ inches (8.9 cm) in diameter. Cut the circle in half (photo 1). Roll each half-circle into a cone shape and glue the narrow end with the fabric adhesive (photo 2). Do the same for the other piece.

PHOTO 1

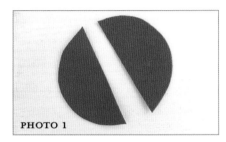

PHOTO 2

2 Cut two 4½ inch (11.4 cm) pieces of brass chain with your wire cutters.

3 Open the loop on an eye pin with your chain-nose pliers. Find the center link in one of the chain pieces and then move over three links. Connect that link to the eye pin, so the chain's ends hang unevenly, as illustrated in photo 3.

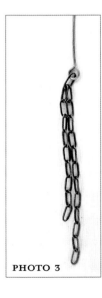

PHOTO 3

PHOTO 4

4 Slide one of the suede cones onto the eye-pin wire, followed by one of the larger brass flower bead caps (photo 4).

PHOTO 5

5 Make beaded dangles. String three head pins each with a blue 5 x 1.5-mm glass bead and a brass textured spacer. String two additional head pins each with a seed bead, a brass lantern-shaped bead, and another seed bead. Connect all of these at various points along the chain piece with wrapped or simple loops (photo 5).

6 Add a 6-mm brass bead cap, a blue 5 x 1.5-mm glass bead, and a textured brass spacer onto the eye pin above the red cone (photo 6). Finish the end with a wrapped loop.

PHOTO 6

7 Open the loop on a lever back ear wire and attach it to the wrapped loop piece (photo 7).

PHOTO 7

Repeat steps 3 through 7 to complete the second earring.

daisy

A ring of wrapped wire loops
reminds me of the playful
petals on a daisy. The red polka
dot-like seed beads add to the
fun in this pair.

procedure

1 Set the pegs into the jig as positioned in photo 1. Cut a 10-inch (25.4 cm) length of silver wire and use the round-nose pliers to create a simple loop. Place the loop over the top peg in the jig (photo 1).

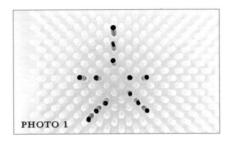

PHOTO 1

2 Maneuver the wire counter-clockwise, as shown in photo 2, around the two pegs to the left and down to the next set of three pegs. Continue going around the pegs and then on to the next set until you have created a floral petal pattern, returning back to the loop at the top (photo 3).

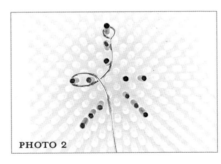

PHOTO 2

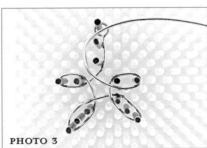

PHOTO 3

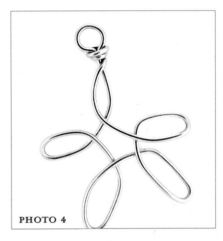

PHOTO 4

3 Remove the flower shape from the pegs and close the shape by making several wraps around the base of the loop. Use the wire cutters to trim any excess wire (photo 4).

Make adjustments to the petal shapes with your fingers and get them just how you like.

PHOTO 5

4 Lay the wire flower on a steel block and hammer the petals with the round end of the chasing hammer (photo 5).

MATERIALS

16 red seed beads, 11°
Silver wire, 20-gauge
Brass wire, 28-gauge
2 decorative French ear
    wires with spiral,
    1 inch (2.5 cm) long

TOOLS

Wire cutters
Round-nose pliers
Jewelry jig with pegs
Chasing hammer
Steel block

DIMENSIONS

2½ x 1¼ inches
    (6.4 x 3.2 cm)

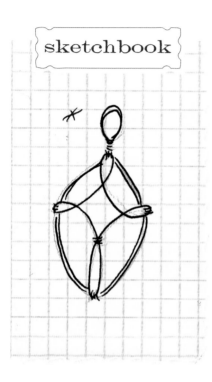

5 Wrap one of the lengths of brass wire securely around the center of the flower. String eight red seed beads, spaced irregularly, onto the wire's free end (photo 6).

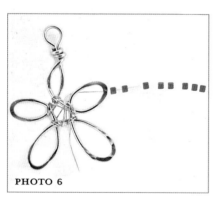

PHOTO 6

PHOTO 7

6 Wrap the brass wire around the center of the flower in a random pattern. Once the wire builds up, work in the red seed beads sporadically (photo 7).

PHOTO 8

7 To finish, thread the end of the brass wire into the back of the flower and trim the end (photo 8).

8 Open the loop on the flower and connect it to one of the ear wire findings (photo 9).

PHOTO 9

Repeat these steps to make the second earring.

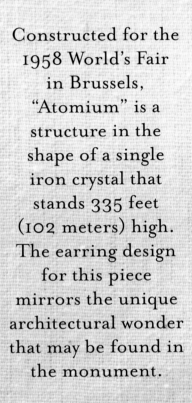

Constructed for the 1958 World's Fair in Brussels, "Atomium" is a structure in the shape of a single iron crystal that stands 335 feet (102 meters) high. The earring design for this piece mirrors the unique architectural wonder that may be found in the monument.

atomium

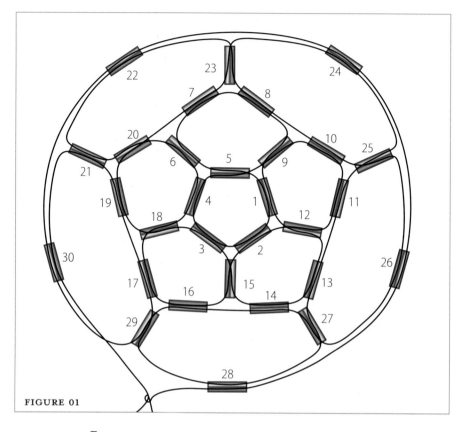

FIGURE 01

MATERIALS

30 blue bugle beads
30 teal twisted bugle
   beads
Silver-colored chain with
   1.5-mm links
2 jump rings, 5 mm
2 French ear wires
Nylon thread, 0.25 mm

TOOLS

Wire cutters
Clear, multipurpose
   jeweler's cement
   with a precision
   applicator tip

DIMENSIONS

3¼ inches (8.3 cm) long

procedure
small bead ball

1 Cut 20 inches (50.8 cm) of the nylon. Pair the ends so you have a "right thread" and a "left thread."

2 String five of the blue bugle beads onto the left thread. Cross the right thread through the fifth bead strung and pull on the thread ends, to make a penta-gram (photo 1). These are beads 1 through 5 in figure 1.

PHOTO 1

3 String four beads (beads 6, 7, 8, and 9) onto the left thread. Cross the right thread through bead 9 and tighten the beads on the thread, to make another pentagon shape.

4 Pass the right thread through bead 1. String three beads (beads 10, 11, and 12) onto the left thread. Cross the right end through bead 12 and snug the beads to make a pentagon shape.

5 Pass the right thread through bead 2. String three beads (beads 13, 14, and 15) onto the left thread. Cross the right thread through bead 15 and snug the beads into shape.

6 Pass the right thread through bead 3. String three beads (beads 16, 17, and 18) onto the left thread. Cross the right thread through bead 18 and snug the beads.

7 Pass the right thread through beads 4 and 6. String two beads (beads 19 and 20) onto the left thread. Cross the right thread through bead 20 and snug the beads. The strung beads will take on a domed shape.

PHOTO 2

8 Pass the right thread through bead 7. String three beads (beads 21, 22, and 23) onto the left thread. Cross the right thread through bead 23 and snug the beads (photo 2).

9 Pass the right thread through beads 8 and 10. String two beads (beads 24 and 25) onto the left thread. Cross the right thread through bead 25.

10 Pass the right thread through beads 11 and 13. String two beads (beads 26 and 27) onto the left thread. Cross the right thread through bead 27.

11 Pass the right thread through beads 14 and 16. String two beads (beads 28 and 29) onto the left thread. Cross the right thread through bead 29.

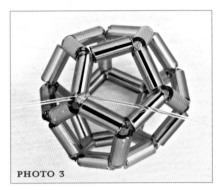

PHOTO 3

12 String one bead (bead 30) onto the left thread. Pass the left thread through beads 22, 24, 26, and 28. Pass the right thread through beads 17, 19, 21, and 30. Tie the two tails together with a tight knot. Secure the knot with a dab of cement. You now have a small blue bead ball (photo 3).

larger bead ball

13 Cut a new piece of nylon thread 20 inches (50.8 cm) long. Use the teal bugle beads to make a second beaded bead by repeating steps 2 through 12. Before closing this new ball entirely, drop the small beaded bead inside (photo 4). Finish the beaded bead by tying it off.

PHOTO 4

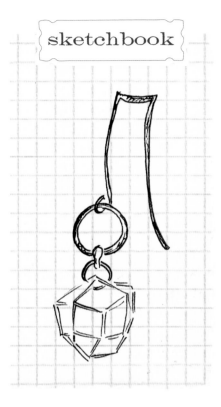

14 Open the jump ring on an ear wire. Cut a section of chain three inches long. Thread one end through the large beaded bead. Bring both ends together and connect them to the jump ring (photo 5).

PHOTO 5

Repeat steps 1 through 14 to make the second earring.

life

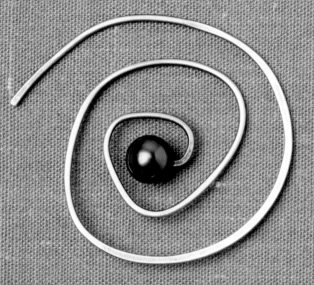

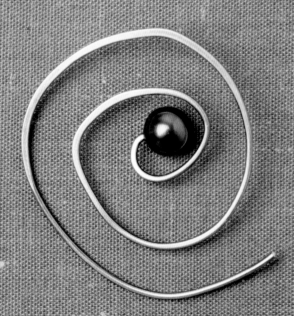

MATERIALS
2 half-drilled black
    pearls, 6 mm
Half-hard sterling wire,
    20 gauge
Liver of sulfur (optional)

TOOLS
Wire cutters
Round-nose pliers
Bench block
Chasing hammer
Brass brush (optional)
Cup burr tool
Clear, multipurpose
    jeweler's cement
    with a precision
    applicator tip

DIMENSIONS
1¼ inches (3.2 cm)
    in diameter

The spiral is a symbol that represents
our journey of life. I love creating spirals.
They are both harmonious and peaceful.

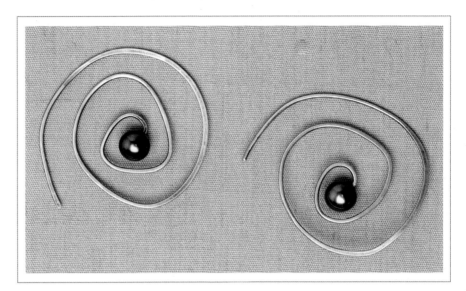

procedure

1 Cut two 4-inch (10.2 cm) pieces of wire. Use your round-nose pliers to start a spiral at the ends of the wires (photo 1). Continue forming an open, irregular spiral with your thumb and index finger (photo 2) for each wire.

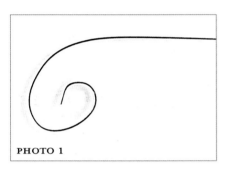

PHOTO 1

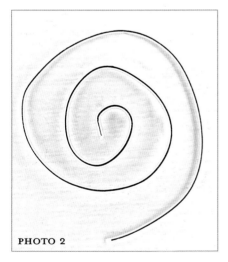

PHOTO 2

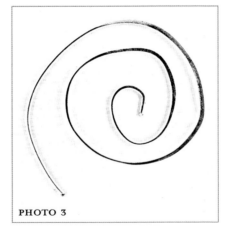

PHOTO 3

2 Hammer the spirals on the steel block with the flat face of the chasing hammer (photo 3).

Optionally, you can apply a liver of sulfur patina to the spirals. See page 19 in the Basic Techniques section.

3 Apply one or two drops of jeweler's cement to one of the wire's ends (in the middle of the spiral), and slide a pearl into place (photo 4). Set it aside to dry. Repeat with the other spiral.

PHOTO 4

4 Round the ends of the wires with a cup burr tool, or smooth them with sandpaper.

MATERIALS

6 blue gemstone
   briolette beads,
   5 x 2 mm
6 brass spacer beads
   with textured rim,
   4 mm
Half-hard silver wire,
   20 gauge
Gold-filled wire,
   22 gauge
6 silver balled head
   pins, 24 gauge,
   2 inches (5.1 cm) long

TOOLS

Wire cutters
Chain-nose pliers
Round-nose pliers
Steel bench block
Chasing hammer
Dowel rod or mandrel,
   ½ inch (1.3 cm)
   in diameter
Sandpaper or cup burr

DIMENSIONS

1½ x ⅝ inches
   (3.8 x 1.6 cm)

twirled

Twist and wrap, round and round;
then find your hammer and block. In the end
you have this pretty little pair of earrings
for nearly any occasion.

procedure

1 Cut a piece of silver wire 7 inches (17.8 cm) long and twirl one end of it into a spiral 1 inch (2.5 cm) in diameter. Spirals are organic shapes, so don't worry if yours isn't perfectly round. This design is meant to be playful.

Make a right-angle bend in the straight tail. Flatten just the spiral on a steel bench block, using the flat face of your chasing hammer (photo 1).

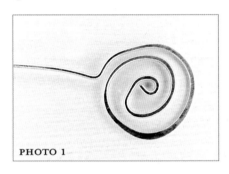

PHOTO 1

2 Close up the outermost ring of the spiral by wrapping a piece of gold-filled wire four to six times around it, as shown in photo 2. Trim the excess gold wire and tuck in the tails with the chain-nose pliers.

PHOTO 2

sketchbook

3 Form the tail end of the silver wire around the mandrel to create the ear wire. Trim the wire to your desired length and smooth its end with sandpaper or a cup burr. You can tweak the hook shape at the end of it with the chain-nose or round-nose pliers. Also, I like to flatten that small section of ear wire that's just before the ear lobe curve with the flat part of the chasing hammer, to work harden it (plus, it looks cool!) See photo 3.

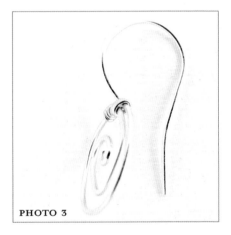

PHOTO 3

4 String one blue bead and a brass spacer bead onto a head pin. Connect the dangle to the bottom of the spiral with a wrapped loop (photo 4). Connect two more of these wrapped dangles to the spiral.

PHOTO 4

Repeat these steps to make the second earring.

MATERIALS

2 buttons or rivolis,
    14 mm
2 brown faceted glass
    beads, 8 mm
2 brass bezel links,
    20 x 14 mm
2 brass head pins,
    2 inches (5.1 cm)
2 brass bead caps, 5 mm
2 French ear wires

TOOLS

Wire cutters
Chain-nose pliers
Round-nose pliers
Alcohol ink and felt pad
    (optional)
Very soft brass brush
    (optional)
Clear, multipurpose
    jeweler's cement
    with a precision
    applicator tip

DIMENSIONS

1¾ x ½ inches
    (4.4 x 1.3 cm)

button love

I'm a sucker for a button box buried in an antique store. These glass, shell, and resin buttons were part of a mixed lot I found in just such a store—right next door to my studio. It was quite a score!

sketchbook

procedure

1 Adhere a button to one of the bezel links with the multi-purpose cement (photo 1). I like to nestle my bezel pieces in a bed of uncooked rice while they dry, so they can sit evenly.

PHOTO 1

PHOTO 2

2 All of the brass findings were too bright and brassy compared to the buttons, so I toned them down by rubbing them with a felt pad infused with brown alcohol ink (photo 2).

PHOTO 3

3 String a glass bead and bead cap onto a head pin. Finish with a simple loop (photo 3). Open the loop and attach it to one of the loops on the bezel link. This dangle will be at the bottom of your new earring.

PHOTO 4

4 Open the loop on an ear wire and connect it to the other (top) loop on the bezel link (photo 4).

Repeat steps 1 through 4 to make the second earring.

TIP

Shine up dull metal buttons by using dish soap and brushing them with a soft brass brush (photo 5). Take care to dry them well because some buttons rust.

PHOTO 5

VARIATION

gearhead

A design that combines textured metal and rubber suggests to me a sort of industrial-chic look: sleek and lean, but with a little bit of sass.

MATERIALS

2 large-holed Bali silver
  disks with basket-
  weave texture
2 large-holed antiqued
  brass bead spacers,
  15 mm
Copper metallic
  rubber cord, 1 mm
  in diameter
Brushed-finish brass
  chain, 5-mm links
Brass wire, 25 gauge
2 brass ear wires,
  with coil and
  bead elements

TOOLS

Wire cutters
Chain-nose pliers

DIMENSIONS

2¾ x ¾ inches
  (7 x 1.9 cm) long

procedure

1 Using wire cutters, cut two pieces of brass chain, each three inches (7.6 cm) long. Also cut two 3-inch pieces of rubber cord.

2 Thread the tail end of one cord through a disk and a bead spacer. Fold the tail up so it's alongside the other part of the cord. Wrap the paired cord six or seven times, just above the disk and spacer, with brass wire, as shown in photo 1. Trim away any excess rubber and wire with the cutters.

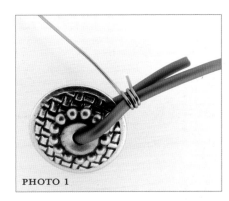

PHOTO 1

3 Start weaving the rubber cord through each link of one of the chain pieces (photo 2). Push the cord down toward the discs as you weave to make it look crumpled. This will result in ¾ inch (1.9 cm) of scrunched chain.

PHOTO 2

4 As an option, I added a liver of sulfur patina to the ear wires so they would harmonize with the rustic finishes of the components.

5 Then I looped the rubber cord through an ear wire and secured it by wrapping another piece of brass wire around the paired portion of the rubber (photo 3). Trim away any excess rubber and wire with the wire cutters.

PHOTO 3

Repeat these steps 2 through 4 to make the second earring.

grow

I didn't get a green thumb, but I like the idea of growing things and having plants around my home. These little green droplets of sparkle make me think of seeds, so I surrounded them with my favorite leaf micro-charms.

procedure

1 Use the wire cutters to cut a 1¾-inch (4.4 cm) length of chain.

2 From the leftmost link on the chain piece, connect a leaf charm with a jump ring. Skip a link; then hang one of the CZ briolettes (photo 1). Continue this connection process until you have used a total of seven leaves and six CZ drops. The right-hand end should have an empty link or two.

PHOTO 1

Optionally, you can apply a patina to the entire earring with a solution of liver of sulfur (see page 19 in the Techniques section). The post earrings I used in this design were already oxidized (photo 2).

PHOTO 2

3 Use a jump ring and the chain-nose pliers to connect the empty link at one end of a chain to the butterfly nut (photo 3). Connect the chain's other end to the loop of an ear post with a jump ring.

PHOTO 3

Repeat these steps to make the second earring.

simple

MATERIALS

Aluminum sheet, 22
   gauge, 4 x 4 inches
   (10.2 x 10.2 cm)
2 gunmetal square links,
   5 mm
2 gunmetal kidney ear
   wires
Purple acrylic enamel
   paint
Alcohol inks and metallic
   paints
Acrylic spray varnish

TOOLS

Jewelry shears
Metal letter punch set
Steel bench block
Hammer
Rawhide mallet
Sandpaper, 400-grit
Small metal hole punch
Paintbrushes

DIMENSIONS

2 x ⅜ inches (5.1 x 1 cm)

Stamping on sterling silver
gives me a bit of anxiety,
so I use aluminum instead.
With its cost-friendly price,
if I mess up, I grab
another piece and try
again. Simple, right?

procedure

1 Using the jewelry shears, loosely cut two rectangular shapes of equal size (1⅜ x ⁵⁄₁₆ inches, 3.5 x 0.8 cm) from the aluminum sheet.

2 Lay one of the aluminum pieces on the steel bench block. Use the hammer to stamp the words you want onto it (photo 1).

PHOTO 1

If the aluminum curled during the stamping process, flatten it on the steel block with the rawhide mallet. Sand the corners and sides of the metal pieces with sandpaper, to remove the rough, cut edges.

3 Punch a hole for the ear wires at the top of the metal piece.

4 Brush a thick layer of purple enamel paint into the recessed areas of the aluminum. Wipe away the excess with a paper towel, leaving only the letters filled with the paint. Set the piece aside to dry (photo 2).

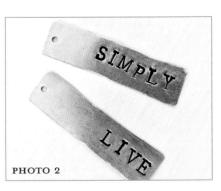

PHOTO 2

sketchbook

PHOTO 3

5 Decorate the surface with metallic paints and alcohol inks. I like to add one layer at a time. Using a dry-brush technique, highlight the edges with a bold color—for these I used teal (photo 3). Seal the pieces with a coat of acrylic spray varnish, to protect the painted surface.

6 Connect the ear wire to the finished, sealed piece. For an extra decorative element, hang a square link in front of the metal piece as you put it on the wire (photo 4).

PHOTO 4

Repeat steps 2 through 4 to complete the second earring.

Rope, framed by scallops and seashell drops, suggests a nautical theme, which reminds me of billowing sails as a tall-masted ship sets out to explore dreams and discover new frontiers.

MATERIALS
2 teal glass shell beads,
   6 x 2 mm
2 silver scalloped-edge
   rectangular findings,
   35 mm long, with
   3.8 mm channel depth
2 silver pinch bails, 10 mm
4 silver head pins,
   2 inches (5.1 cm)
2 smooth silver spacer
   beads, 5 mm
2 round ear wires,
   with ball
Teal rope, ¼ inch (0.6 cm)
   in diameter

TOOLS
Wire cutters
Chain-nose pliers
Round-nose pliers
Scissors
Clear, multipurpose
   jeweler's cement
   with a precision
   applicator tip

DIMENSIONS
3 x 9/16 inches (7.6 x 1.6 cm)

anchors away

procedure

1 With the scissors, cut a piece of the rope to fit inside the rectangular finding (photo 1). Dab the ends of the rope with the cement, to prevent it from fraying. Set the rope piece aside.

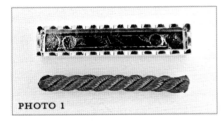

PHOTO 1

2 Attach a pinch bail to a glass shell bead, using the chain-nose pliers to close each prong into a hole on the glass bead, as shown in photo 2. This is a shell dangle.

PHOTO 2

3 At one end of the rectangular finding, insert a head pin from the inside.

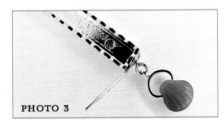

PHOTO 3

4 Use a wrapped loop to finish the end of the head pin, making sure to connect the shell dangle before closing up the loop (photo 3).

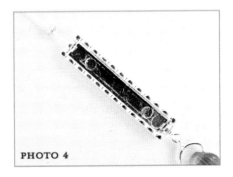

PHOTO 4

5 String a second head pin through the other end of the rectangular finding, starting from the inside; then string a silver spacer bead onto the head pin (photo 4). Trim the wire to ⅜ inch (1 cm) and finish it with a simple loop, formed with round-nose pliers (photo 5).

PHOTO 5

6 Use the multipurpose cement to secure the rope to the inside of the finding frame (photo 6).

PHOTO 6

7 Connect an ear wire to the loop made in step 5 (photo 7), using the chain-nose pliers to open and close the ear wire loop.

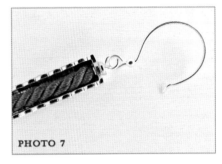

PHOTO 7

Repeat these steps to make the second earring.

VARIATION

MATERIALS

4 square tube garnet
  beads, 7 x 3 mm
4 gunmetal daisy spacer
  beads, 5 mm
2 Bali silver elephant
  charms, 13 x 22 mm
4 solid silver-colored
  twist rings, 6 mm
2 solid brass twist rings,
  9 mm
2 copper three-hole
  daisy spacer bar links,
  10 x 4 mm
4 gunmetal balled head
  pins, 2 inches (5.1 cm)
  long
2 silver-colored jump
  rings, 5 mm
6 silver-colored jump
  rings, 6 mm
Silver wire, 22 gauge
2 silver kidney ear wires,
  35 x 20 mm
Liver of sulfur (optional)
Pumice powder

TOOLS

Wire cutters
Chain-nose pliers
Round-nose pliers
1.5-mm coiling mandrel
Brass brush

DIMENSIONS

2 ½ inches (6.4 cm) long

hatari

My editor emailed me, saying that these earrings
reminded her of the old movie *Hatari*, and included
a link to its Henry Mancini theme song.
As a big fan of Mancini's *Breakfast at Tiffany's* soundtrack,
I got hooked on *Hatari* too.

procedure

1 Cut a 36-inch (91.4 cm) piece of silver wire and use the coiling mandrel to wrap it into a coiled length of 3 inches (7.6 cm), as shown in photo 1.

PHOTO 1

2 Cut the coiled section in half with wire cutters. Slide a coiled piece over each of the kidney ear wires, so it sits in the front-facing area, as illustrated in the right side of photo 2.

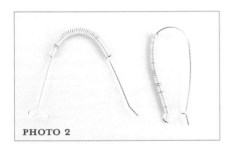

PHOTO 2

3 Optionally, you can apply a liver of sulfur patina to the ear wire and coil (photo 3). Rub the coil with pumice to remove the patina and highlight the coil's texture. Brush the wires with a brass brush and dish soap to make them shiny again.

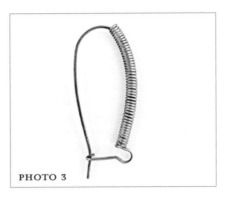

PHOTO 3

4 String one garnet bead and one gunmetal daisy spacer onto a balled head pin; finish the head pin with a simple loop and trim any excess wire. Connect this dangle to a small silver-colored twist ring. Create another dangle with another garnet bead, daisy spacer, balled head, and silver-colored twist ring.

5 Connect one of the elephant charms to the copper three-hole bar with a 5-mm jump ring.

6 Connect each of the garnet dangles and the elephant dangle to one of the 9-mm twist rings, using one 6-mm jump ring for each dangle, as shown in photo 4.

PHOTO 4

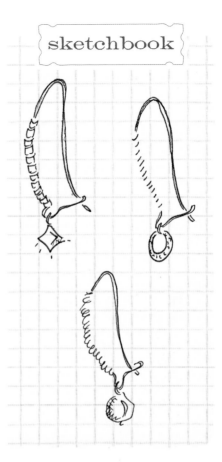

7 Slide the brass ring into the loop of one of the ear wires. Push the bottom-hook part of the ear wire up enough to close the loop a little, securing the brass ring in place (photo 5).

PHOTO 5

Repeat steps 5 through 7 to complete the second earring.

MATERIALS

2 teal oval glass beads,
20 x 15 mm

2 faceted gold glass
beads, 5 x 3 mm

2 purple crystal
bicones, 4 mm

2 faceted teal beads,
8 mm

4 oxidized brass fold-
over crimps, 9 mm

2 oxidized textured
brass bead caps,
8 mm

2 oxidized brass head
pins, 22 gauge,
2 inches (5.1 cm)

6 oxidized brass jump
rings, 6 mm

2 triangle jump rings,
14 x 15 mm

16 oxidized brass jump
rings, 5 mm

Kidney ear wires, 18 mm

Silver leather braid,
⅛ inch (0.3 cm) wide

TOOLS

Wire cutters

Chain-nose pliers

Round-nose pliers

DIMENSIONS

2⅞ x ⅞ inches
(7.3 x 2.2 cm)

band of braid

This silver leather is chic and rustic at the same
time. As a collector of cowboy boots, I happen to
love the idea of an "urban cowgirl." This design
is for all of the urban cowgirls out there!

procedure

1 Cut two lengths of the leather braid, each 2½ inches (6.4 cm) long. Finish the four cut ends with the fold-over crimp findings (photo 1).

PHOTO 1

2 String a large oval teal bead, a textured bead cap, a faceted gold bead, and a purple bicone onto the head pin; then finish it with a wrapped loop. Open a 6-mm jump ring with the chain-nose pliers and attach it to the wrapped loop (photo 2).

PHOTO 3

PHOTO 2

3 Open a triangle jump ring and string the crimped end of a leather piece onto it (photo 3).

4 Now you'll place more findings on the triangle. Because it opens in the center of one side, you may have to do some juggling when putting them on, but follow this order from left to right:

- 5-mm jump ring
- 6-mm jump ring
- three 5-mm jump rings
- the teal bead dangle
- three 5-mm jump rings
- 6-mm jump ring
- 5-mm jump ring
- the other crimped end of the leather

Close the triangle jump ring with your chain-nose pliers (photo 4).

PHOTO 4

5 Open the kidney ear wire and hang the triangle jump ring on it; then slide a faceted teal bead onto the wire so it sits at the front (photo 5).

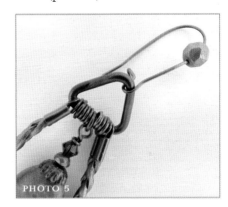

PHOTO 5

Repeat steps 2 through 5 to complete the second earring.

curry in a hurry

This pair of earrings brings the exotic locale of India to my mind. For festive flair, the design uses curry-colored recycled sari silk and colorful beads.

MATERIALS

16 iridescent brown faceted Czech beads, 4 mm

6 iridescent red faceted Czech beads, 4 mm

2 red Czech rose petal glass beads, 14 x 13 mm

4 silver spacer beads, 5 mm

2 brass barrel beads, 4 x 4 mm

24 silver balled head pins, 1 inch (2.5 cm)

2 Bali silver chandelier earring findings with bars and loops, 1 inch (2.5 cm) in diameter

2 silver eye pins, 2 inches (5.1 cm)

2 Bali silver diamond-faceted earring posts with loops, 12 x 9.6 mm

2 silver jump rings, 5 mm

Silver wire, 24 gauge

Gold sari silk, ½ x 8 inches (1.3 x 20.3 cm)

TOOLS

Wire cutters

Chain-nose pliers

Scissors

Clear, multipurpose jeweler's cement with a precision applicator tip

DIMENSIONS

2⁵⁄₁₆ x 1 inches (5.9 x 2.5 cm)

procedure

1 String one faceted Czech bead onto each of the 24 head pins. Finish each dangle with a simple loop.

2 Connect the dangles you made in step 1 to the loops in the chandelier findings, as follows: 2 brown, 1 red, 1 brown, 1 red, 2 brown, 1 red, 1 brown, 1 red, 2 brown (photo 1).

PHOTO 1

3 Use your chain-nose pliers to remove the jump rings that connect the paired bar pieces to the chandelier findings, leaving the bar pieces connected to each other. Set aside the two jump rings you opened for a later project. Repeat the process for the other chandelier finding.

PHOTO 2

4 Cut the sari silk into four pieces, each measuring ½ x 2 inches (1.3 x 5.1 cm). Glue the end of a silk piece to one of the bars. Wrap the material around it; then glue that end down too (photo 2).

PHOTO 3

Make several wraps of silver wire at one end of the silk-wrapped bar, wrap it down along the bar, and finish at the other end with several more wraps, as illustrated in photo 3. Cover the other three bars in the same way.

PHOTO 4

5 Open the loops on both of the eye pins. Attach a rose petal bead to each (photo 4). String a silver spacer bead, a brass barrel bead, and another silver spacer bead onto each of the eye pins. Finish each pin with a loop and trim any excess wire (photo 5).

PHOTO 5

6 Connect one of the dangles you made in step 5 to the jump ring that connects a pair of silk-covered bars. Connect the remaining dangle to the other pair of silk-covered bars in the same way (photo 6). Then reconnect the bar pairs to the chandelier findings.

PHOTO 6

7 Use a 5-mm jump ring to attach an embellished chandelier to the loop on one of the earring posts, as shown in photo 7. Do the same for the second earring.

PHOTO 7

MATERIALS

68 round coral beads*, 1.5 mm

2 teal Czech glass faceted beads, 4 mm

22 blue gem chip beads*, 4 mm

38 teal seed beads*, 13°

2 silver bead frames, ¼ inch (6 mm) in diameter

2 silver bezel frames, 1 inch (2.5 cm) in diameter

2 decorative silver French ear wires

Nylon thread

*You may need to adjust your bead counts to suit the bezel frame you have.

TOOLS

Wire cutters

Chain-nose pliers

Fine-tip tweezers

Clear, multipurpose jeweler's cement with a precision applicator tip

DIMENSIONS

1¾ x 1 inches (4.4 x 2.5 cm)

rain dance

The silver used with these colorful concentric circles lends a sense of the American Southwest. I think of a desert environment and the desire for rain.

procedure

1 Cut 4 inches (10.2 cm) of nylon thread and string 15 of the coral beads onto it. Thread one end through the first two beads again, to make a ring. Before pulling the tails of nylon to snug up the ring, set a bead frame inside the coral ring to check the fit (photo 1).

PHOTO 1

2 Measure and mark the center point of the bezel. Apply cement to the middle of a bezel and place one of the bead frames there; then place a faceted teal bead inside the silver frame. Next, set the beaded ring from step 1 around the bead frame (photo 2).

PHOTO 2

3 Add more cement onto the bezel in the space around the coral beads. Use tweezers to drop 11 gem chips into the bezel (photo 3).

PHOTO 3

4 Cut another length of nylon thread 4 inches (10.6 cm) long. String 19 coral beads and the same number of teal seed beads onto the nylon so they alternate; you may need more if the circumference of your bezel is different. Thread the end of the tail through the first two beads to create a ring (photo 4).

Trim the excess nylon thread. Put a few beads of cement around the outside ridge of the bezel that you've been working on and set the striped ring in place. Leave it to dry.

PHOTO 4

PHOTO 5

5 Open the loop on an ear wire and attach the bezel charm to it (photo 5).

Repeat steps 1 through 5 to make the second earring.

doily

These miniature colorful doilies were so sweet.
I had to find out if they could
be wire-wrapped onto a hoop earring!

MATERIALS

2 crocheted doilies,
    each 1½ inches
    (3.8 cm) or less in
    diameter
1 pair silver hoop
    earrings, each
    1½ inches (3.8 cm)
    outer diameter
Silver wire, 28 gauge
Vinegar
Alcohol ink in a
    desired color*

*I used purple ink.

TOOLS

Paintbrush
Scissors
Clear, multipurpose
    jeweler's cement
    with a precision
    applicator tip

DIMENSIONS

1½ inches (3.8 cm)
    in diameter

procedure

I've been finding lots of tiny doilies in the scrapbooking section of my local craft store. This is a fun way to put them to use.

dye the doilies

1 Working on a nonabsorbent surface, such as a plate, use a paintbrush to saturate the outer edges of your doilies with vinegar.

2 Put drops of the colored alcohol ink around the outer edges of the doilies. The color will bleed toward the centers. Push on the edges with the end of a paintbrush to make the ink bleed more, until you see the effect you want (photo 1).

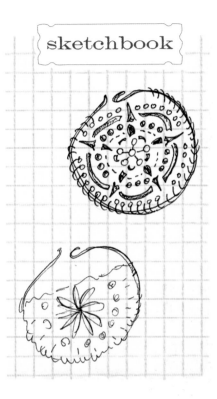

PHOTO 2

3 Put the doilies in a microwave oven for 20 seconds to set the dye (photo 2). Use a hair dryer to finish the drying completely if you want to work with the doilies right way. I like to set mine in a mesh bag over a vent so they dry in a couple of hours.

wrap them

4 Use the scissors to cut a piece of wire 10 inches (25.4 cm) long. Secure one end to an earring hoop (where it won't interfere with the mechanisms) with a few wraps. Position a doily in the center of the hoop and stitch it to the ring with the wire. Optionally, you can add decorative wraps in between the doily stitches (photo 3).

PHOTO 1

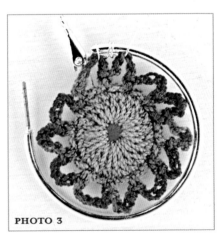

PHOTO 3

5 Stitch the doily all the way around the hoop. Secure the wire when completed with a few wraps before trimming the excess (photo 4). For extra security, put a drop of the multipurpose cement on the ends of the wires to keep them tucked in.

PHOTO 4

Repeat steps 4 and 5 with the remaining doily to make the second earring.

MATERIALS
2 pink flatback crystals,
    4 mm
Seed bead assortment
    in your desired color
    palette*
Orange ball chain
2 silver-toned,
    perforated domed
    discs, 1 inch (2.5 cm)
    in diameter
2 Bali silver spacer
    beads, 12 mm
2 clip-on earring
    findings
Cherry-colored silk
    ribbon, ¾ inches
    (1.9 cm) wide
Sewing thread to
    complement the silk
    ribbon/cord
3-inch square of red
    acrylic felt

*I used two bead
    colors: iridescent
    cherry and clear
    glass lined with
    bright plum

MATERIALS
2 pink flatback crystals,
    4 mm
Seed bead assortment
    in your desired color
    palette*
Orange ball chain
2 silver-toned,
    perforated domed
    discs, 1 inch (2.5 cm)
    in diameter
2 Bali silver spacer
    beads, 12 mm
2 clip-on earring
    findings
Cherry-colored silk
    ribbon, ¾ inches
    (1.9 cm) wide
Sewing thread to
    complement the silk
    ribbon/cord
3-inch square of red
    acrylic felt

*I used two bead
    colors: iridescent
    cherry and clear
    glass lined with
    bright plum

TOOLS
Wire cutters
Needle
Scissors
Clear, multipurpose
    jeweler's cement
    with a precision
    applicator tip

DIMENSIONS
1 inch (2.5 cm)
    in diameter

strawberry jam

Sweet and swirly like strawberry freezer jam!
Mmm! Stitch and bead your heart out with this
pair of earrings, my dears!

procedure

1 Cut 18 inches (45.7 cm) of thread. Thread the needle; bring the two tails together and tie a knot there. Anchor the thread to each of the base discs (photo 1). Cut 6 inches (15.2 cm) of ribbon into ¼-inch (0.6 cm) strips.

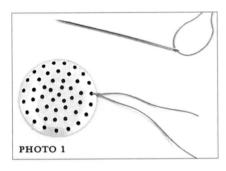

PHOTO 1

2 Stitch half of the ribbon pieces all the way around a disc's edge, using the threaded needle. I like to twist the ribbon as I go, to make it thicker (photo 2). Don't be concerned about stray threads, as they add an interesting textural effect.

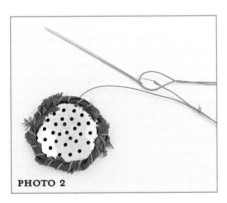

PHOTO 2

PHOTO 3

3 Stitch a section of ball chain to the disc, just inside the ribbon's perimeter, and add extra stitches in between each ball (photo 3). When you make a full circle, trim the chain and add a touch of cement to connect the ends.

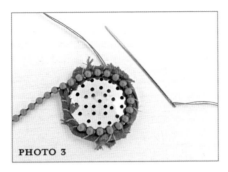

PHOTO 4

4 Next, stitch one seed bead at a time (colors as desired), in two concentric rings, inside the ring of the ball chain (photo 4). If you wish, you may make patterns by alternating different-colored seed beads.

5 Finish the center of the earring by stacking a flatback crystal on top of a spacer bead (see opposite page). A clothespin works well for clamping these elements to the disc while they dry (photo 5).

PHOTO 5

6 Cut a small circle of red felt to fit the back of the silver disc and secure it with the multipurpose cement. That will cover any scary stitch lines! Adhere a clip-on finding to the back of the felt piece with the cement (photo 6). For pierced earrings, use a post earring finding with a glue pad.

PHOTO 6

Repeat steps 2 through 6 to finish the second earring.

tropicana

Big, bold, and saucy!
This pair will shake things up
like a night on the town.

MATERIALS

46 pink stone nugget
  beads, 5 to 6 mm
14 wooden beads, 5 mm
12 green faceted Czech
  glass beads, 5 mm
Green copper wire
  ribbon, 20 mm wide
2 silver hoops, 3 inches
  (7.6 cm) in diameter
2 oxidized and ham-
  mered brass rings,
  13 mm in diameter
Green wire, 26 gauge
Silver wire, 20 gauge
Nylon filament
2 brass French ear wires

TOOLS

Wire cutters
Chain-nose pliers
Round-nose pliers
Clear, multipurpose
  jeweler's cement
  with a precision
  applicator tip

DIMENSIONS

3⅜ x 2⅝ inches
(8.6 x 6.7 cm)

procedure

1 Cut a length of wire ribbon 7 ½ inches (19 cm). Fold it lengthwise and wrap it around the outer edge of a hoop. As illustrated in photo 1, the ends should overlap by no more than ¼ inch (0.6 cm).

PHOTO 1

2 Secure the section of over-lapping wire ribbon with the green wire. Poke the wire down through both layers, and then back up again (photo 2). Take two more stitches; then trim the wires to ⅛ inch (0.3 cm). Roll the trimmed ends under.

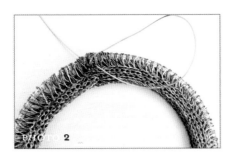

PHOTO 2

3 String 23 of the pink beads onto the silver wire. Form this beaded wire into a circle small enough to fit just inside the ribbon-covered hoop.

PHOTO 3

4 Trim the silver wire so you leave a tail 1 inch (2.6 cm) long (photo 3). Cross one tail over the other, leaving a space of ¼ inch (0.6 cm) between the first and last beads. Wrap the tails onto the beaded wire, tucking in the last bit of the ends.

PHOTO 4

5 Using the nylon thread, string six of the wooden beads and six of the green glass beads in an alternating pattern. Finish with a last wooden bead and then a brass ring, as shown in photo 4.

PHOTO 5

6 Knot the beads around both the ribbon-covered hoop and the pink ring of beads (photo 5). Dot the knot with a touch of cement.

PHOTO 6

7 Open the loop on a French ear wire and connect it to the brass ring (photo 6).

Repeat these steps to make the second earring.

Some of the first jewelry pieces I made back in high school were from hemp, using macramé techniques. Here I am, 18 years later, making macramé jewelry. Funny, how everything eventually circles back around.

MATERIALS

- 2 copper rondelle beads with AB crystals, 6 mm
- 2 flatback AB crystals, 4 mm
- 4 blue flatback crystals, 3 mm
- 2 copper teardrop pendants with loops, 1 ¾ x 1 inches (4.4 x 2.5 cm)
- 2 copper filigree flowers, 15 mm
- 6 copper oval jump rings, 6 x 4 mm
- 2 decorative filigree lever back ear wires, with loops
- Blue nylon multifilament cord

TOOLS

- Wire cutters
- Scissors
- Beading needle with collapsible eye
- Tape
- Clear, multipurpose jeweler's cement with a precision applicator tip

DIMENSIONS

- 2 ½ x 1 inches (6.4 x 2.5 cm)

bohemian chic

procedure

A half-hitch knot is traditionally used in macramé designs. Instead of hemp, we will cover the pendant frame with half-hitch knots made from relatively delicate nylon cord. The knotting pattern alternates, to create a flat ribbon. If you were to repeat the same knotting motion throughout the process, you would create a twist instead of a flat ribbon edge.

1 To utilize the half-hitch knotting technique, cut the nylon cord so you have two pieces that each measure 1½ yards (1.4 m). Tape one side of the copper pendant to a steady surface.

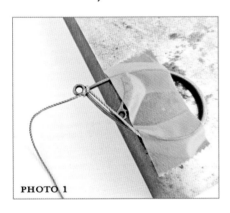

PHOTO 1

Tie one end of a piece of cord at the top of the pendant, next to the loop. The cord now has a longer, working end and also a shorter tail of about 1 inch (2.5 cm), as shown in photo 1.

2 You'll work with the longer tail of the cord to do the knotting. First, shape the longer tail so the long end goes over the top of the pendant's wire frame and also over the tail. Now, put the

PHOTO 2

working end of the cord through the pendant and back up through the new loop in the cord (photo 2). Tighten the cord. This is the first knot path.

3 Now for the second knot path. Bring the longer end of the tail under the pendant's wire frame, up through the pendant, over the tail and the frame, and then down through the inside of the new loop, as shown in photo 3. Pull out the slack, sliding your knots up toward the starting point. After a few more knots, the tail will be covered.

PHOTO 3

4 Now, alternate using the knot paths from steps 2 and 3 (photo 4), until you have covered the entire hoop with half-hitch macramé. When you reach a separating bar on the pendant's frame, just work a knot around it.

PHOTO 4

5 Tie off the end of the cord and add a drop of cement to secure the last knot (photo 5).

PHOTO 5

PHOTO 6

6 Thread the needle with an 8-inch (20.3 cm) strand of cord. Use it to add a laced edge around one of the filigree lever back ear wires (photo 6). Tie off the ends and secure with cement.

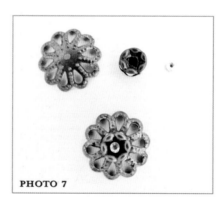

PHOTO 7

7 Use the multipurpose cement to attach a rondelle to the center of one of the filigree flowers, and adhere the clear AB flatback crystal to the center of the rondelle (photo 7).

Connect the flower to the middle loop inside the pendant with an oval jump ring. Use the multi-purpose cement to attach blue flatback crystals to the loops that flank either side of the jump ring (photo 8).

PHOTO 8

Attach the copper teardrop link to the ear wire with a pair of oval jump rings (photo 9).

PHOTO 9

Repeat these steps to make the second earring.

rain forest

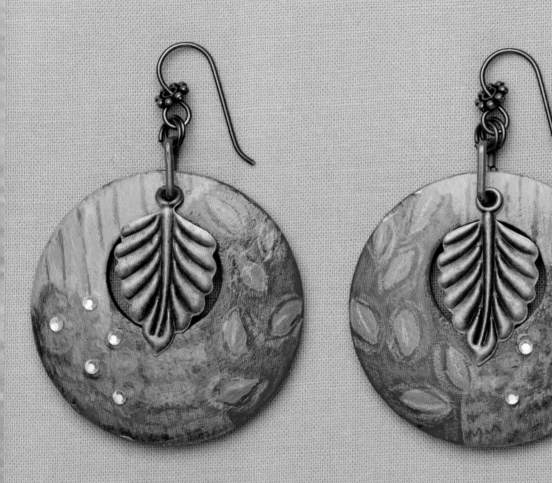

These earrings were inspired
by the mental image
of birds creating trails of vibrant colors
as they streak through the rain forest.
Someday I want to go there and see them for myself!

MATERIALS

2 wood hoops, 1¾ inches
in diameter

10 AB flatback crystals,
1 mm

2 brass leaf charms,
25 x 15 mm

2 brass square jump rings,
9 mm

4 brass round jump rings,
5 mm

2 niobium ear wires,
color to match or
complement your
color scheme

2 brass daisy spacer
beads, 5 mm

Acrylic paints in colors
of your choice

Acrylic varnish,
semi-satin finish

Decoupage medium,
matte finish

TOOLS

Wire cutters
Round-nose pliers
Fine-grit sandpaper
Paintbrush
Oil-based colored
pencils, quantity and
colors of your choice
Clear, multipurpose
jeweler's cement
with a precision
applicator tip

DIMENSIONS

2¼ x 1⅝ inches
(5.7 x .6 cm)

sketchbook

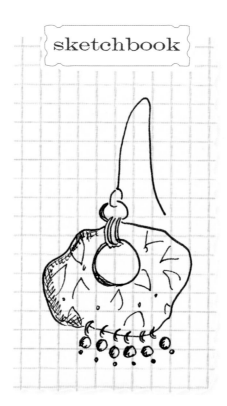

procedure

1 If the wood hoops have a finish on them, sand them lightly with fine-grit sandpaper to create a tooth on the surface. Wipe them clean (photo 1).

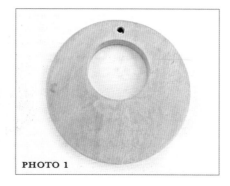

PHOTO 1

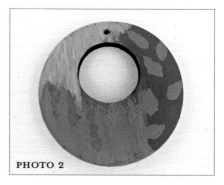

PHOTO 2

2 Paint the wood hoops however you like, adding dots, squiggles, and blocks of color. Simple forms and designs work best (photo 2).

PHOTO 3

3 Use colored pencils on the surface to highlight the painted shapes and add dimension to them (photo 3). If you like, see how your paints and pencils will look by testing them first on a similar scrap of wood. Oil pencils allow for blending, so experiment by coloring light colors on top of dark ones.

4 Seal the colored hoops with the varnish and leave them to dry (photo 4).

PHOTO 4

5 Add crystals to the surfaces of the hoops, using the decoupage medium as an adhesive. I like to dip the wooden end of my paintbrush in the medium and then touch it to the hoop surface to make perfect dots of glue (photo 5).

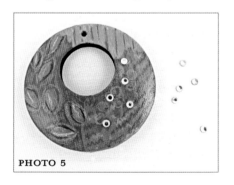
PHOTO 5

PHOTO 6

6 Open one of the square jump rings and use it to connect one of the leaves, a hoop, and two of the round jump rings (photo 6).

7 Use the round-nose pliers to open the loop on an ear wire and connect it to the two small jump rings on the component you made in step 6. Secure the daisy spacer just above the loop on the ear wire with the jeweler's cement (photo 7).

PHOTO 7

Repeat steps 6 and 7 with the other hoop to make the second earring.

I love choosing an image or design to transfer onto these little blank shell bead canvases.

artistic roundabout

procedure

1 Size and print four copies of a favorite image onto the transfer film with an inkjet printer (photo 1). This type of transfer product can be found online or at craft stores.

PHOTO 1

2 Following the manufacturer's instructions, adhere the image to both sides of the shell bead (photo 2). Use small scissors to trim away any excess film from the shell bead.

PHOTO 2

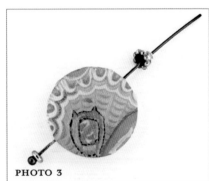

PHOTO 3

3 String a silver spacer bead, one of the decorated shell beads, and a bead cap onto each of the head pins (photo 3). Finish by making a simple loop on each pin.

PHOTO 4

4 Open the simple loops and connect each dangle to an ear wire (photo 4). Trim the excess wire.

Repeat these steps to make the second earring.

framed

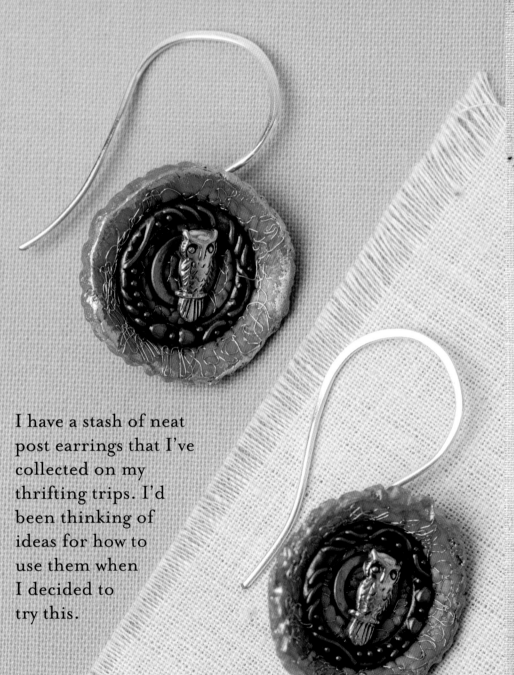

I have a stash of neat
post earrings that I've
collected on my
thrifting trips. I'd
been thinking of
ideas for how to
use them when
I decided to
try this.

MATERIALS

1 pair of stud earrings
   with post nuts
Tiny beads, rings, wire
   mesh, or objects to
   embed in clay
2-part epoxy clay in
   your favorite color
Metallic paints
Sterling wire, 20 gauge

TOOLS

Wire cutters
Chain-nose pliers
Round-nose pliers
Dowel or jig
Silicone work mat
Rolling pin
Circle clay cutter,
   from ¾ to 1 inch
   in diameter
   (19 to 25.4 mm)
Sandpaper
Wooden skewer,
   slightly larger in
   diameter than the
   stud earrings' posts

DIMENSIONS

1 inch (2.5 cm) in
   diameter

procedure

1 Cut two pieces of sterling wire, each 3 inches (7.6 cm) long and make a small loop at one end of both. Form each length into an ear wire, using a dowel rod or a jig (see the Basic Techniques section, page 14). Sand to smooth any rough ends (photo 1).

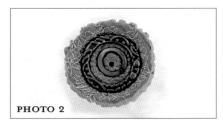

PHOTO 1

2 Mix the epoxy clay according to the manufacturer's instructions; then roll it flat onto the silicone mat.

Embed tiny beads, rings, or other objects into the clay. Cut two circles out of the embellished clay. For this pair, I embedded pieces of delicate wire mesh into the clay, along with a copper ring for each circle. Additionally, you can gild the clay with metallic paints or glazes.

3 Form the edges of the clay circles to give them dimension. Use the wooden skewer to poke a hole in the center of each; this will let you to use different post earrings from your collection at any time. Set the decorated clay circles aside to dry (photo 2).

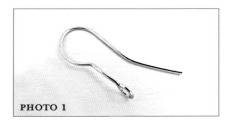

PHOTO 2

PHOTO 3

4 Thread an ear post through a clay disc (photo 3). Place the small loop of the ear wire around the post on the back of the disc; then push the wire above the loop forward, to make a slight bend above your new earring. Secure the wire to the post with a nut (photo 4).

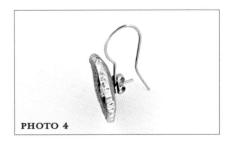

PHOTO 4

Repeat step 4 to make the second earring.

PHOTO 5

Make as many discs as you like to give yourself some options for the basic stud earrings. One pair of ear wires can be used again and again (photo 5).

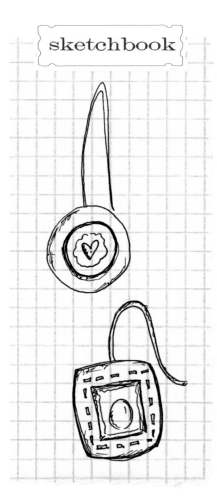

VARIATION

dragonfly tales

My parents have a cottage, where I love watching dragonflies buzz about on long summer days. The various colors on their shimmery wings are absolutely beautiful.

MATERIALS

6 light purple, faceted glass beads, 5 mm
2 antique brass dragonfly-wing beads, 20 x 6 mm
2 black, flat metal pendant discs, 25 mm in diameter
2 gunmetal balled head pins
2 gunmetal jump rings, 6 mm
2 antique brass twisted rings
2 lever back ear wires

TOOLS

Wire cutters
Chain-nose pliers
Round-nose pliers
Green and teal enamel paints
Embossing die in folding holder
Embossing roller mill
Paintbrush
Sanding block

DIMENSIONS

2 x 1 inches (5.1 x 2.5 cm)

procedure

1 Lay one of the metal discs into the holder of an embossing tool used to press texture into flat pieces of metal (photo 1). Follow the manufacturer's instructions to create a patterned metal piece. Repeat the process with the second disc.

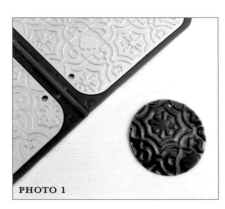

PHOTO 1

2 Paint the pieces with splashes of green and teal enamel paints and set them aside to dry (photo 2).

PHOTO 2

PHOTO 3

3 Sand the embossed surfaces of the painted discs with a sanding block to remove paint from the raised areas (photo 3).

PHOTO 4

4 Make a dragonfly dangle. String two purple beads, a wing bead, and a purple bead onto one of the head pins (photo 4). Finish the end of the wire: use the round-nose pliers to make a wrapped loop; then trim any excess wire with the wire cutters.

5 Use a jump ring to connect one of the twisted rings, a dragonfly dangle, and one of the discs (photo 5). Use the chain-nose pliers to open the loop on a lever back and connect it to the twisted ring (photo 6).

PHOTO 5

PHOTO 6

Repeat steps 4 and 5 to make the second earring.

queen anne

Queen Anne Boleyn comes to my mind, in her fluffy lace collar and wearing delicate pearl and gold earrings. The royal blue color in these, and the lace-like quality of the filigree, makes me wonder if she would have liked them.

procedure

1 Spray the two large filigree pieces in your favorite color (photo 1) and set them aside to dry.

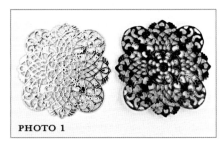

PHOTO 1

2 Use the metal punch to make a small hole in the center of each of these filigree pieces (photo 2).

PHOTO 2

3 Set one of the filigree pieces into the shallow cavity of a wood dapping block. Use the punch to push the center of the filigree piece down into the block's recess (photo 3).

PHOTO 3

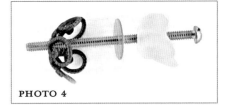

PHOTO 4

4 Check the fit of a sequin and a resin flower to see if they can be strung onto one of the micro-bolts (photo 4). If they don't fit, enlarge their holes using the hole punch for the sequin and the twist drill for the resin flower (photo 5).

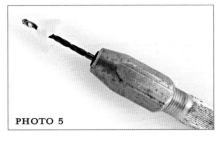

PHOTO 5

5 Onto the bolt, string the resin flower and the sequin, plus a filigree bead cap, a daisy bead cap (concave side first), the silver filigree piece, the blue filigree piece, and the washer onto the bolt. Tighten the nut onto the bolt to secure the layers together.

6 Use the wire cutters to cut the bolt flush with the nut, and smooth any rough edges with a nail file. Add a drop of cement over the nut to ensure it can't loosen later (photo 6).

PHOTO 6

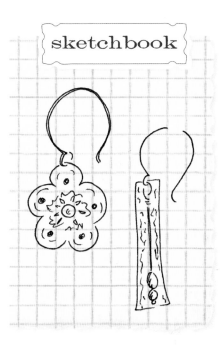

7 String a daisy spacer and a small brass bead onto an ear wire and finish one end with a loop (photo 7).

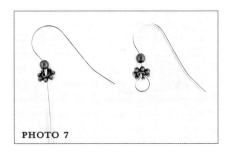

PHOTO 7

8 Open the loop and connect the filigree piece to it (photo 8).

PHOTO 8

Repeat steps 3 through 8 to finish the second earring.

EARRINGOLOGY

love lines

Tiny brass hearts dangling at the ends
of delicate chains made me think of lines
that end in symbols of love, because I grew up
watching Dr. Drew's TV show, *Loveline*.

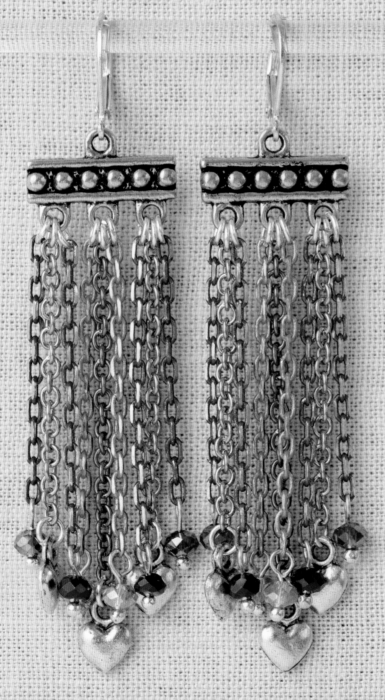

MATERIALS

4 blue metallic finish
glass faceted rondelle
beads, 3 x 4 mm

4 teal metallic finish
glass faceted rondelle
beads, 3 x 4 mm

4 purple metallic finish
glass faceted rondelle
beads, 3 x 4 mm

6 gold heart charms,
6 mm

12 brass balled head pins,
2 inches (5.1 cm) long

Blue chain, 2-mm links

Blue diamond-cut chain,
2-mm links

Teal chain, 2-mm links

Purple diamond-cut
chain, 2-mm links

Teal diamond-cut chain,
2-mm links

24 brass jump rings,
5 mm

2 brass three-hole end
bars, ¾ inches (1.9 cm)
long

2 brass lever back
ear wires

Note: The chain lengths
are a little longer
than you'll need; a
small amount of
chain will be lost
due to cutting it.

TOOLS

Wire cutters
Chain-nose pliers
Round-nose pliers

DIMENSIONS

3 x 1 inches (7.6 x 2.5 cm)

procedure

1 String a rondelle bead onto a balled head pin and finish the dangle with a simple loop, using the round-nose pliers. Repeat for all of the beads (photo 1).

PHOTO 1

2 Cut two 2-inch (5.1 cm) lengths of blue chain. In addition, cut four pieces each of the following:

- blue diamond-cut chain, each 1¼ inches (3.2 cm) long
- teal chain, each 1⅜ inches (3.5 cm) long
- purple diamond-cut chain, each 1½ inches (3.8 cm) long
- teal diamond-cut chain, each 1¾ inches (4.4 cm) long

3 Using a jump ring, connect one of the blue diamond-cut chain pieces to a left-side loop on one of the end bars. Connect a piece of teal chain to the same loop, followed by a purple diamond-cut chain, again using a jump ring for each (photo 2).

PHOTO 2

PHOTO 3

4 As shown in photo 3, use jump rings to connect a teal diamond-cut chain, blue chain, and teal diamond cut chain to the center loop. Repeat chain attachments on the right loop, mirroring the pattern of the left loop.

PHOTO 4

5 Using photo 4 as a guide, connect a heart charm with a 5-mm jump ring to the free ends of the center chains on each of the three loops. Next, connect a beaded dangle to match the color of each of the remaining chains (e.g., a purple rondelle to the purple chain, teal to teal, and so on).

6 Attach an ear wire to the loop at the top of the end bar (photo 5).

PHOTO 5

Repeat steps 3 through 6 to make the second earring.

VARIATION

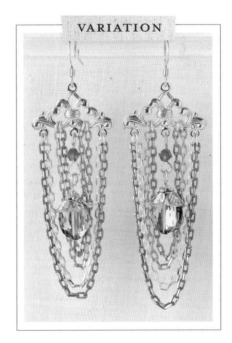

ranch land

I was inspired by the earth tones and loose structure of the grouped cords. They make me think of horseback rides and the beautiful scenery of rolling ranch land.

MATERIALS

20 copper seed beads, 3 mm

2 spacer beads, 3 mm

4 copper daisy spacers, 5 mm

2 turquoise bead chips, 2 x 8 mm

2 silver bead cones, 16 x 6 mm

Round leather cord, 1 mm in diameter

Nylon-coated, tarnish-resistant alloy 7-strand beading wire, .015 in silver

Hand-painted rayon gimp*

Silver wire, 24 gauge

2 silver head pins

2 silver French ear wires

*Fabric cord with a wire in the center of it

TOOLS

Wire cutters

Chain-nose pliers

Round-nose pliers

Clear, multipurpose jeweler's cement with a precision applicator tip

DIMENSIONS

3½ x 1¼ inches (8.9 x 3.2 cm)

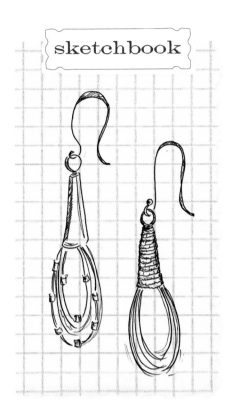

procedure

1 Cut 4-inch (10.2 cm) lengths of the following:

- Three pieces of leather cord
- Three pieces of beading wire
- Four pieces of gimp

Make three or four groups of two pieces, combining a leather or gimp piece with a beading wire. Slide two large copper seed beads over these to hold them together. The remaining single pieces get one seed bead (photo 1). You can choose to let these beads slide freely along the

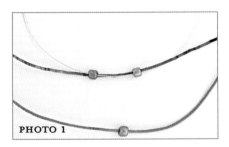

PHOTO 1

cords (where they will invariably end up at the bottom of the loop you will be forming), or glue them where you want them, so they stay in place.

NOTE

This really can be an "anything goes" type of step when it comes to grouping the wire, gimp, and leather. Feel free to mix and match these materials in any way you wish.

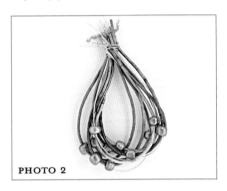

PHOTO 2

2 Bring the ends together for all the pieces from step 1 and bind them with a short length of silver-colored wire (photo 2).

3 String a 3-mm spacer bead and a silver cone onto a head pin (photo 3).

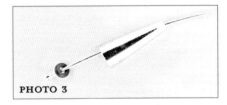

PHOTO 3

4 String a copper daisy spacer, a turquoise chip, and another copper spacer onto the head pin. Finish the pin with a wrapped loop. Trim any excess wire with the wire cutters.

PHOTO 4

Glue the bound ends of the cords (from step 2) into the cone, using the jeweler's cement (photo 4).

5 Connect one of the ear wires to the wrapped loop you just made, using the chain-nose pliers to open the loop (photo 5).

PHOTO 5

Repeat these steps to make the second earring.

TIP

Create a matte finish on the ear wires by rubbing them with water and pumice powder. This will help them match the copper seed beads (photo 6).

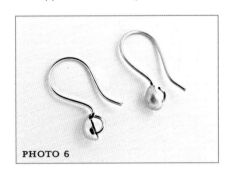

PHOTO 6

Do you have treasured clip-on earrings from a beloved relative that pinch your lobes so hard you don't ever want to wear them? Me, too! I've got a quick and easy way to refashion vintage clip-ons. And here's the best part: they won't pinch your ears anymore.

treasured

MATERIALS

2 vintage beaded
   clip-on earrings
2 copper AB crystal
   rondelles, 6 mm
6 brass spacer beads,
   5 mm
2 brass bead caps and
   flatback crystals
Gold-filled wire,
   20 gauge

TOOLS

Wire cutters
Chain-nose pliers
Round-nose pliers
Cup burr or sandpaper
Mandrel, ½ inch (1.3 cm)
   in diameter
Clear, multipurpose
   jeweler's cement
   with a precision
   applicator tip

DIMENSIONS

2⅛ x 1⅛ inches
   (5.4 x 2.9 cm)

procedure

1 Use your wire cutters to remove the clip from the back of the vintage beaded earring. Get the tip of the cutting tool as close to the flat part of the back as you can (photo 1).

PHOTO 1

2 If you choose, you can hide the cut section by gluing in a fancy bead cap and crystal (photo 2). This is the kind of detail that I love so much when making custom jewelry!

PHOTO 2

3 Cut a 3-inch (7.6 cm) length of gold-filled wire and use the round-nose pliers to make a loop at one end. Use the chain-nose pliers to open the loop and pass

PHOTO 3

it through the outermost ring of beads on the earring. It may take a little finagling. String an assortment of spacer beads onto the wire; I used a brass spacer, a crystal rondelle, and two more brass spacers (photo 3).

PHOTO 4

4 Make a 90-degree bend in the wire and bend the section nearest the spacer beads over a mandrel, into the shape of a French ear wire (photo 4). Reposition the mandrel so you can curve the end of the wire in the opposite direction. Hammer the side of the ear wire and round the wire ends with a cup burr tool or smooth them with sandpaper.

Repeat these steps to make the second earring.

sketchbook

nested

Nests made from
bugle-bead strands
create a frame for the
chunky beads in this design.
I love this technique because
it looks complicated—when it's
actually very simple!

procedure

1 Open the loops on each of the ear wires with chain-nose pliers and set a brown faceted bead in place. Pinch the wires closed to keep the bead securely in place (photo 1).

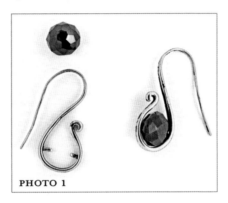

PHOTO 1

2 String 70 brass bugle beads onto a length of nylon thread.

PHOTO 2

3 Slide seven of the beads toward one end of the nylon thread. Tie a knot in the nylon to form the group into a ring (photo 2) and trim the thread ends with scissors. Repeat the process with

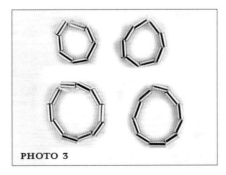

PHOTO 3

another seven beads. Then make a ring with eight of the beads; repeat. Make four more rings, each with 10 beads. You will have two sets of brass bugle-bead rings, each having a seven-bead ring, an eight-bead ring, and two ten-bead rings (photo 3).

4 On a head pin, string
  • a large brown acrylic bead
  • a set of beaded rings from step 3 (from biggest to smallest)
  • a gray and gold lampworked bead
  • a 5-mm bead cap

PHOTO 4

Finish the end of the wire with a simple loop as shown in photo 4. Repeat the stringing with the other head pin to make a second dangle.

PHOTO 5

5 Open one of the loops and connect it to the bottom of an ear wire (photo 5). Attach the other dangle to the other ear wire in the same way.

stripes & type

One of my all-time favorite practices is to incorporate stripes into my art;
they are so playful and bold! Here are some stripes made from type and gold paint.
The random letters make me imagine these earrings are hiding cryptic messages!

MATERIALS

2 hoop earrings,
    2 inches (5.1 cm) in
    diameter, with
    outer tracks
Assorted metal rings,
    ½ to 1 inch
    (1.3 to 2.6 cm) in
    diameter
Black leather strip
Gold paint
Decoupage medium,
    matte finish
Dictionary paper

TOOLS

Small paintbrush
Small, sharp scissors
Clear, multipurpose
    jeweler's cement
    with a precision
    applicator tip

DIMENSIONS

2½ x 2 inches
    (6.35 x 5.1 cm)

procedure

1 To determine how much leather will be needed, lay it in the outer track of one of the hoops, and then cut it as shown in photo 1. Remove the leather and apply cement to the recessed area of the hoop; then press the leather back into place.

PHOTO 1

2 Paint small vertical stripes in gold onto the leather; then set it aside to dry.

3 Cut tiny pieces of dictionary paper to fit on top of the leather, inside the recessed area of the hoop. Following the manufacturer's instructions, use the decoupage medium to adhere bits of cut paper all the way around the leather. Set it aside to dry (photo 2).

PHOTO 2

4 Slide three or four rings in order, from largest to smallest, onto the hoop (photo 3). Because of their size, they probably won't stay in that order, but that's what makes these fun!

PHOTO 3

Repeat these steps to make the second earring.

MATERIALS

8 nugget heishi silver spacer beads, 6.7 mm

10 nugget heishi silver spacer beads, 5 mm

8 brass spacer beads, 5 mm

2 gunmetal pendant findings with 9 loops, 2 inches (5.1 cm) long

18 gunmetal jump rings, 6 mm

2 gunmetal jump rings, 5 mm

2 hammered-texture post findings with loops, 13.3 x 7.3 mm

TOOLS

Chain-nose pliers

DIMENSIONS

2½ x 1⅜ inches (6.4 x 3.5 cm)

koi pond

These metal shapes remind me of scales on a fish. The movement of the beads creates flashes of light, just like glistening water.

procedure

1 Open a 6-mm jump ring with the chain-nose pliers; then hang a brass spacer and one of the larger heishi spacer beads on it (photo 1). Repeat three times.

PHOTO 1

2 Connect this ring to the center-bottom loop in the pendant finding, as shown in photo 2.

PHOTO 2

PHOTO 3

3 Add another of these bead dangles to each of the loops above the center-bottom one, and also to the topmost loop (photo 3).

PHOTO 4

4 Fill in the remaining spaces in the pendant with 5-mm heishi nuggets on 6-mm jump rings (photo 4).

5 Connect the pendant to the post finding with a 5-mm jump ring (photo 5).

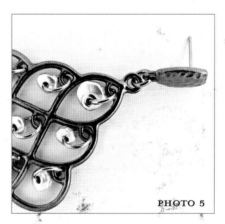

PHOTO 5

Repeat these steps to make the second earring.

earthenware

MATERIALS

52 dark moss agate
  beads, 4 mm

48 orange andesine
  beads, 4 mm

8 copper crimp
  beads, 1°

4 three-hole beaded-
  edge spacer bars

2 four-hole beaded-
  edge spacer bars

2 gunmetal eye pins,
  2 inches (5.1 cm)*

2 oval hammered-
  copper links,
  18.5 x 13 mm

2 beaded-edge spacer
  beads, 5 mm

2 copper hexagon
  spacer beads,
  4.3 mm

2 copper ear wires with
  silver coil detail

19-strand nylon-coated
  copper beading wire,
  0.018 inch

*Or make your own
  from 2-inch (5.1 cm)
  pieces of 24-gauge
  wire.

TOOLS

Wire cutters
Chain-nose pliers
Round-nose pliers

DIMENSIONS

2⅝ x 1⅝ inches
  (6.7 x 4.1 cm)

I used simple glass and
stone beads in rich terra
colors, plus coppery findings,
to create this
multi-textured look.

procedure

1 String one copper crimp bead, a dark moss agate bead, and an orange andesine bead onto the copper beading wire. String another dark bead, then an orange bead. Repeat twice more, and then pass the wire through an end hole in a three-hole spacer bar.

2 Continue the stringing: put an orange bead, a dark bead, an orange bead, a dark bead, and an orange bead onto the wire, followed by another three-hole spacer bar (through an end hole).

3 Next, string an orange bead and a dark bead onto the wire. Repeat this sequence three more times; follow with a copper crimp bead.

PHOTO 1

4 Cross both wire tails through the second hole in a four-hole spacer bar so they cross each other; there should be a crimp bead on either side of the spacer bar. Pull the tails snug (photo 1); then crimp the copper beads with the chain-nose pliers. Trim the tails of the wire to complete the ear-ring's inner ring.

5 Cut an 8-inch piece of the beading wire for the second (outside) ring. Thread it, counter-clockwise, through the adjacent (third) hole in the four-hole spacer bar. String a copper crimp bead onto it, followed by five sequences of alternating a dark bead with an orange bead; then add one last black bead.

6 Thread the wire through the outside hole in the three-hole spacer bar that is attached to the inner circle. Alternate dark and orange beads three times; then add another dark one.

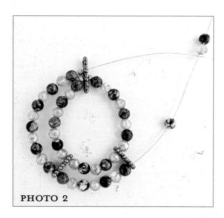

PHOTO 2

7 Take the wire through the outside hole of the next three-hole spacer bar (photo 2) and string a dark and orange bead sequence five times, followed by a dark bead and a copper crimp bead.

PHOTO 3

8 Thread the tails through the hole in the four-hole spacer bar where you started this second ring, and through the crimp beads on either side of the spacer, so that the tails cross, as shown in photo 3. Remove the slack and flatten the crimp beads with your chain-nose pliers. Trim the excess wire.

9 Open the loop on an eye pin and hang an oval copper link on it. You may need to make the loop a little larger with your round-nose pliers to get the link to hang nicely. String a beaded spacer bead and a copper hexagon bead onto the pin and finish it with a loop (photo 4).

PHOTO 4

PHOTO 5

10 Open the loop you just made and hang the oval dangle from the inside hole of the four-hole spacer bar (photo 5). Attach a copper ear wire to the topmost hole on that spacer bar (photo 6).

PHOTO 6

Repeat these steps to make the second earring.

set in slate

...or faux slate, in this instance! The silvery, shimmery, porous surface of the stone veneer makes it a superb base layer for attaching a multitude of materials, giving a multidimensional look.

MATERIALS

2 engraved shell pieces,
¾ inch (2 cm) in
diameter

24 rondelles, 5 x 3 mm

1 sheet of slate veneer
in silver

6 brass jump rings, 6 mm

1 spool of brass wire,
24 gauge

12 brass balled head pins,
2 inches (5.1 cm)

2 brass post earring
findings with loops

TOOLS

Wire cutters

Chain-nose pliers

Round-nose pliers

Pencil

Heat gun

Rotary drill and #55 bit

Sandpaper, 320-grit

Heavy-duty scissors
or snips

Clear, multipurpose
jeweler's cement
with a precision
applicator tip

DIMENSIONS

3¼ x 1⅛ inches
(8.3 x 2.9 cm)

procedure

1 Lay a shell piece on top of the slate veneer, and use the pencil to draw a circle ⅛ to ¼ inch (3 to 6 mm) larger than the shell onto the slate. Warm the slate piece with a heat gun. Cut out the slate circle with heavy-duty scissors or snips (photo 1). Repeat the process for the second shell piece.

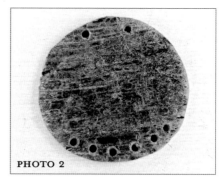

PHOTO 2

PHOTO 1

2 Sand the edges of the slate circles. Drill two holes, ½ inch (1.3 cm) apart, at the top of each piece; then drill six more holes along the bottom, 1 mm from the edge and ³⁄₁₆ inch (5 mm) apart (photo 2).

PHOTO 3

with brass jump rings, as shown in photo 5. Glue a round shell to the center of a slate circle and set it aside to dry.

PHOTO 5

PHOTO 7

3 String one rondelle onto the tail of the spool of 24-gauge wire. Finish the tail with a simple loop and trim the excess wire. Still working on the spool, create a wrapped loop on the other end of the bead. Bring the wire over the bead and back to your first loop, then around it a few times. Trim the wire to separate that wrapped bead link from the spool. Repeat the process twice more, connecting each new wrapped bead link to the previous one at the simple-loop end, as shown in photo 3. Each earring will need a pair of these three-bead link sections (photo 4).

PHOTO 4

Repeat this connection and linking technique for the other pair of three-bead link sections.

4 Connect two of these three-bead link sections to the top of one of the slate circles

5 String the remaining 12 rondelles onto the head pins, one bead per pin. Finish each beaded head pin with a simple loop (photo 6).

PHOTO 6

6 Attach six of the beaded head pins to the holes you drilled along the bottom edge of a slate-and-shell piece (photo 7).

7 Open a jump ring with the chain-nose pliers. Use it to connect the paired ends of the bead-link sections to the loop on one of the post earring findings (photo 8).

PHOTO 8

Repeat steps 4, 6, and 7 to finish the second earring.

Create your own ocean tide with this wire mesh ribbon. In between waves, you can nestle tiny crystals that are like shells washing up with the surf.

silver surf

MATERIALS
40 bicone crystals, 3mm
Silver wire mesh ribbon,
  ⅜ inch (1 cm) wide
2 hoop earrings,
  1⅛ inches (2.9 cm)
  in diameter
Silver craft wire,
  24 gauge
Nylon thread

TOOLS
Wire cutters
Chain-nose pliers
Scissors
Clear, multipurpose
  jeweler's cement
  with a precision
  applicator tip

DIMENSIONS
1½ inches (3.8 cm)
  in diameter

procedure

1 Start with one of the wire mesh pieces, which you can cut to a length of 9 inches (22.9 cm) with scissors (photo 1). After opening the latch on one of the hoop earrings, slide the entire mesh as a tube over the hoop (photo 2). Be careful not to snag the mesh during this process.

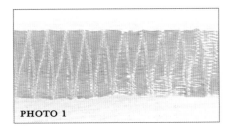

PHOTO 1

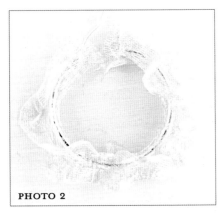

PHOTO 2

2 Secure one end of the mesh next to the hoop closure by tightly coiling 1 inch (2.5 cm) of wire over the top (photo 3). Trim the wire and tuck the ends with the chain-nose pliers. Do the same at the opposite end.

PHOTO 3

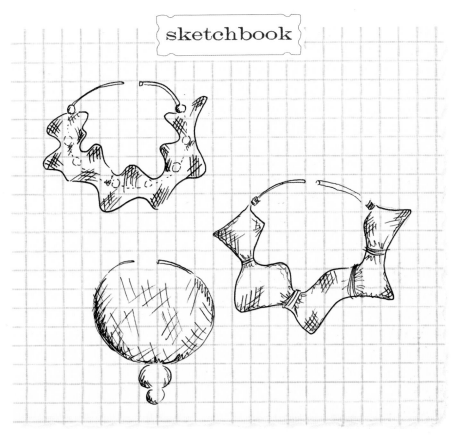

3 Pull the sides of the mesh apart to create waves around the hoop.

4 String four crystals onto the nylon thread; then cinch the thread around the mesh-covered hoop, between waves (photo 4). I started at the bottom center and worked my way around

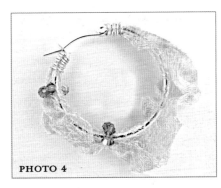

PHOTO 4

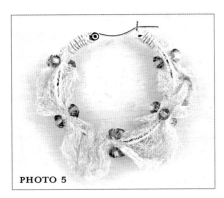

PHOTO 5

the outer edges (photo 5). Add four more crystal cinches in the same way. You can make these sections symmetrical or asymmetrical.

5 Secure each knot with a touch of cement.

Repeat all steps to make the second earring.

for lace lovers

I unearthed a bag of smashed lace
one morning as I rummaged
around in an antique store.
Even though the lace was
pretty dingy, I gently washed
it and it turned out
perfect for making a
pair of old-fashioned
button earrings.

MATERIALS

Upholstery button–
   covering kit
Lace trim, 4 x 6 inches
   (10.2 x 15.2 cm)
Enamel spray paints in
   blue and gold
2 silver post earring
   findings with
   adhesive pad
6 flatback crystals,
   4 mm (optional)
2 pearls, 4 mm
   (optional)

TOOLS

Heavy-duty wire
   cutters
Clear, multipurpose
   jeweler's cement
   with a precision
   applicator tip

DIMENSIONS

$7/8$ inch (2.2 cm) in
   diameter

procedure

1 Upholstery buttons are in two pieces. Follow the manufacturer's instructions for how to cut the lace to fit the button tops.

2 Spray-paint the front and back pieces of two upholstery buttons—these were covered with a layer of gold enamel over a layer of blue (photo 1). Set them aside to dry.

PHOTO 1

3 Position a bit of lace over a button face; then put it face down into the kit's button holder (photos 2 and 3).

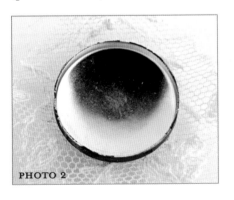

PHOTO 2

PHOTO 3

4 Use heavy-duty wire cutters to remove the shank from the button's back piece. Push the lace down into the recessed area of the button top; then snap the back piece onto it (photo 4). Glue a post over the shank holes, and set the earring aside to dry (photo 5).

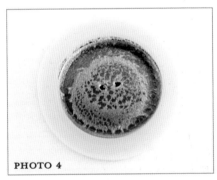

PHOTO 4

PHOTO 5

Repeat the process for the other button back.

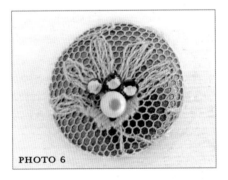

PHOTO 6

Optionally, you can embellish the fronts of these earrings with flat-back gems. Attach them with the multipurpose cement (photo 6).

amethyst fountain

The delicate twisted wires look like streams of water
shooting from an ornate fountain.

procedure

1 Cut a piece of copper wire about 15 inches (38.1 cm) long and string 19 amethyst beads.

2 Leaving a tail of 1½ inches (3.8 cm), separate one of the beads from the others with ⅜ inch (1 cm) of wire between them and make a bend there. Twist this section of wire, as shown in photo 1, from 5 to 10 times.

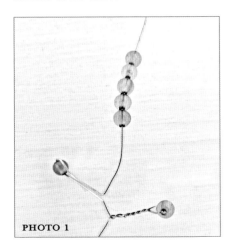

PHOTO 1

Repeat with each of the remaining amethyst beads, leaving ¼ inch (0.6 cm) of wire between each twisted section.

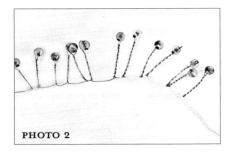

PHOTO 2

3 Leave another tail, 1½ inches (3.8 cm) long, after the last bead (photo 2).

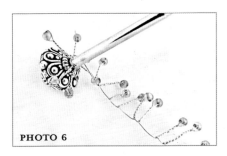

PHOTO 3

4 On one of the silver bead bars, string a 6-mm spacer bead, a 12.5-mm silver bead, and another spacer bead (photo 3).

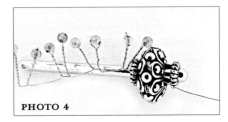

PHOTO 4

Leave a bit of space between the spacer bead and the end of the bar. As shown in photo 4, thread one tail of the wire through the last spacer bead and the large silver bead; then use the rest of the wire to wrap it around the bar in the space between the silver bead and very first spacer bead. Apply a drop of cement to the wrapped area between the first spacer bead and the large bead. Slide the two beads up to the end of the bar (photo 5).

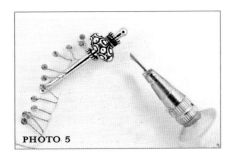

PHOTO 5

5 Wrap the rest of the twisted, beaded wire, including the tail, around the bead bar just above the last spacer bead (photo 6).

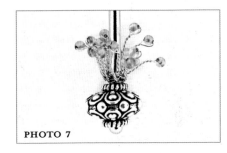

PHOTO 6

Tuck the end of wire in and secure it with cement. Roll the amethyst bead wires outward and down with round-nose pliers (photo 7).

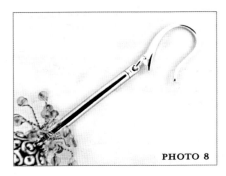

PHOTO 7

6 Connect one of the ear wires to the bead bar with a small jump ring (photo 8).

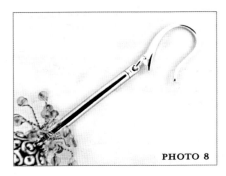

PHOTO 8

Repeat these steps to make the second earring.

MATERIALS

2 light sapphire crystal cup chains, each 3 inches (7.6 cm) long, with 22 crystal links, each 2.5 mm

2 pearl cup chains, each ¼ inch (0.6 cm) long, with 5 links, each 4.1 mm

2 crystal pearls, 8 mm

4 cup chain connectors, 2.5 mm

2 cup chain connectors, 4.1 mm

2 brass bead caps, 6 mm

2 brass balled head pins, 2 inches (5.1 cm) long

2 brass bead caps, 8 x 10 mm

2 brass French ear wires

Brass wire, 24 gauge

Brass wire, 20 gauge

TOOLS

Wire cutters

Chain-nose pliers

Round-nose pliers

DIMENSIONS

2¾ x ½ inches (7 x 1.3 cm)

A bed of pearls within a treasure chest of blue-green sapphire crystals—sparkling like the sea.

sketchbook

procedure

1 Finish each end of one of the sapphire crystal cup chains with a 2.5-mm cup chain connector (photo 1).

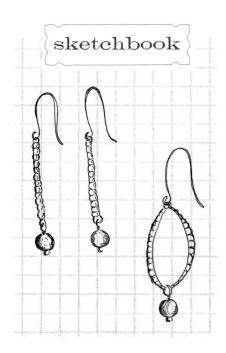

PHOTO 1

2 Match up the connectors' loops so they form the sapphire chain into a teardrop shape. Wrap the 24-gauge brass wire several times around the base of the paired loops to hold the ends together (photo 2). Trim the excess wire and save it for the second earring.

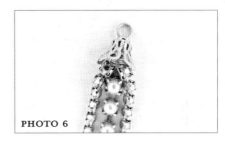

PHOTO 2

3 Finish one end of a pearl cup chain with a 4.1 mm connector (photo 3).

PHOTO 3

4 String a pearl bead and a 6-mm bead cap onto a head pin. Trim the pin so you have an excess of ⅜ inches (1 cm); then finish the head pin with a simple loop. Open the loop and connect it around the bottom of the sapphire chain, between the 11th and 12th crystals (photo 4).

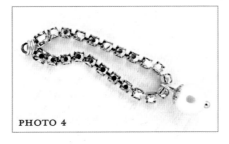

PHOTO 4

Cut two pieces of 20-gauge wire, each 3 inches (7.6 cm) long. Make a loop at the end of one of the pieces. Open the loop and use it to join the connectors for the pearl chain

and the light sapphire chain. Close the loop (photo 5) and save the remaining length of wire for the second earring.

PHOTO 5

5 String one of the larger brass bead caps onto the 20-gauge wire. Finish the end of the wire with a simple loop (photo 6).

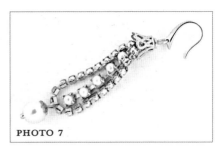

PHOTO 6

Connect one of the ear wires to this loop (photo 7).

PHOTO 7

Repeat steps 1 through 5 to make the second earring.

taj
mahal

It's on my list
of places to see
before I die.
I imagine the
Taj Mahal
to be full of
bright amber
light, ornate
interiors, and
gilding.

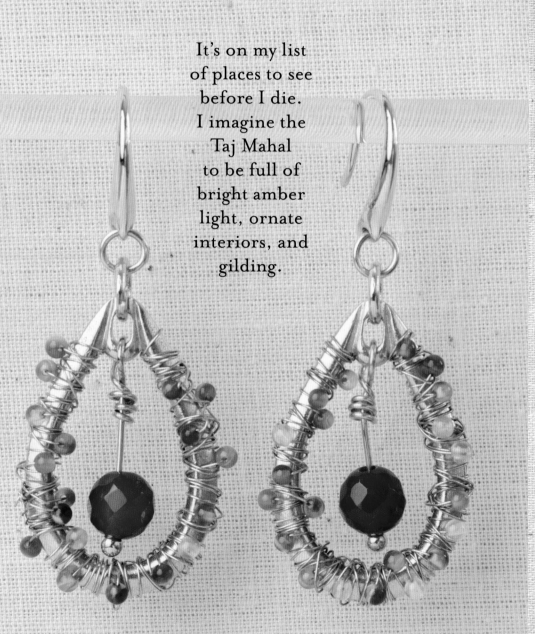

MATERIALS

24 round orange agate
   beads, 2.5 mm
2 orange agate beads,
   6 mm
Brass wire, 28 gauge
2 brass teardrop links,
   18 x 28 mm
2 brass balled head pins
2 brass jump rings,
   6 mm
2 brass jump rings,
   5 mm
2 brass French ear wires

TOOLS

Wire cutters
Chain-nose pliers
Round-nose pliers
Clear, multipurpose
   jeweler's cement
   with a precision
   applicator tip

DIMENSIONS

1⅝ x ¾ inches
(4.2 x 1.9 cm)

procedure

1 Cut a piece of brass wire 12 inches (30.5 cm) long, and string 10 or 12 of the smaller agate beads onto it. I find working with shorter pieces of wire to be easier than a single long piece because it helps to keep the wire from getting a kink in it.

PHOTO 1

2 Secure one end of the wire by wrapping it several times around the top of one of the tear-drop links. As you wire-wrap, slide each bead in place around the link (photo 1). (This process took all of my patience because the beads were so tiny and I wanted them to sit perfectly along the outer edge of the link's profile.)

As needed, cut additional pieces of wire and string them with more beads to complete wrapping around the link.

PHOTO 2

3 Trim the wire and add a couple of drops of jeweler's cement to the backside of the link, where there are loose ends (photo 2). I do this because the wire is very thin and I want to reduce the chance that it might snag or unravel.

PHOTO 3

4 String the 6-mm agate bead onto a balled head pin. Attach the pin to the opening at the top of the teardrop with a wrapped loop. The length of the dangle will depend on how many times you wrap the pin—your choice (photo 3). Trim the excess wire.

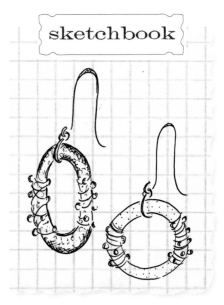

5 Connect one of the larger jump rings to the top of the teardrop. Connect this ring to the ear wire with a smaller jump ring (photo 4).

PHOTO 4

Repeat these steps to make the second earring.

chevron

MATERIALS

34 pink iridescent AB crystal rondelle beads,* 3 x 4 mm

46 purple rondelle glass beads,* 3 x 4 mm

2 pieces of brass square mesh, 1½ inches (3.8 cm)

78 brass head pins, 1 inch (2.5 cm) long

2 brass kidney ear wires with glue pads

*The quantities of rondelle beads needed may be varied, depending on how many you want to add to each mesh piece.

TOOLS

Wire cutters

Chain-nose pliers

Round-nose pliers

Clear, multipurpose jeweler's cement with a precision applicator tip

DIMENSIONS

2¾ x 2⅛ inches (7 x cm)

I had so much fun playing with this aluminum fabric. You could leave it as is or else connect flatback crystals or beaded dangles to it, like I did here!

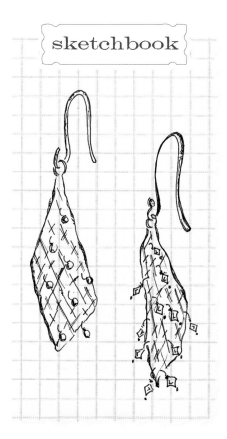

sketchbook

procedure

1 Use the chain-nose pliers to remove one of the flat links from a corner of each of the two mesh pieces, which will reveal a loop. This area will be at the top of the design, where the ear wire will eventually connect to it (photo 1).

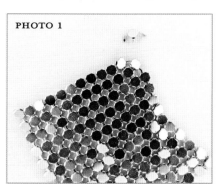

PHOTO 1

2 Apply a drop or two of cement to the glue pads on each ear wire. Attach a pink bead to each one (photo 2).

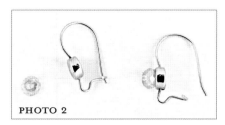

PHOTO 2

3 String one bead onto a head pin and finish it with a simple loop. Do the same with all of the remaining head pins and purple and pink beads.

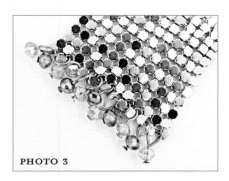

PHOTO 3

4 Create a fringe by attaching half of the beaded head pins to one of the mesh squares, alternating pink and purple rondelles along the bottom sides (photo 3).

Move up four rows on the mesh and connect another row of beads there, between each round element in the mesh. (See the red lines in photo 4 for placement. I placed 13 of the purple rondelles along the longer right-angle.)

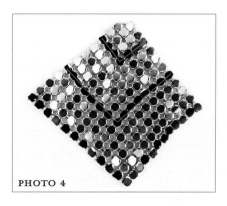

PHOTO 4

Continue step 4 as many times as you like! You could even fill the mesh with beads. For this earring design, I added a row of pink rondelles above the row of purple ones.

5 Hang the beaded mesh piece onto one of the ear wires (photo 5).

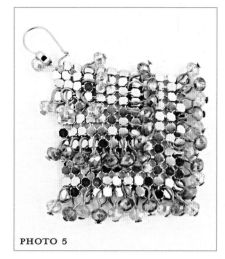

PHOTO 5

Repeat steps 4 and 5 to complete the second earring.

architectural

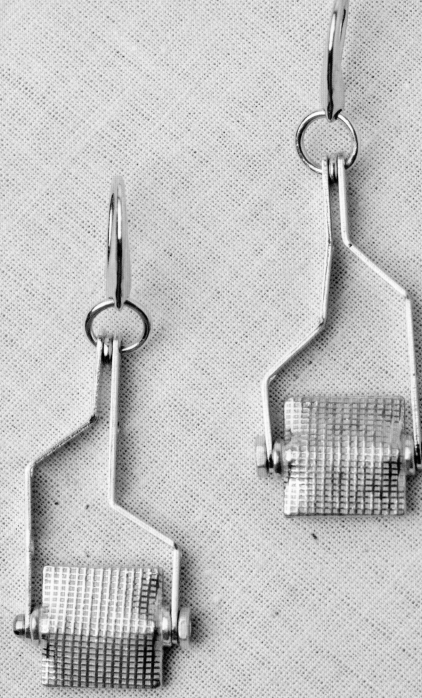

MATERIALS

2 square satin-finish
  vermeil beads,
  14 mm

2 brass spacer disc
  beads, 5 mm

4 brass five-hole spacer
  bars, 2 inches (5.1 cm)
  long

2 micro-bolts with nuts,
  1 inch (2.5 cm) long

2 brass jump rings,
  6 mm

2 brass modern French
  ear wires

TOOLS

Heavy-duty wire
  cutters

Flat-nose pliers

Nail file

Clear, multipurpose
  jeweler's cement
  with a precision
  applicator tip

DIMENSIONS

2⅛ x ¾ inches
  (5.4 x 1.9 cm)

All of these geometric lines!
They take my mind to a grid of city streets
with their skyscrapers jutting out
in all directions.

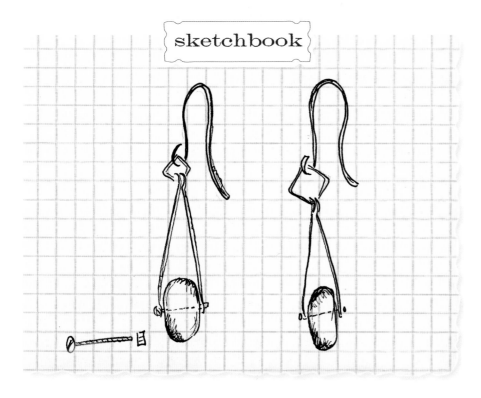

sketchbook

procedure

1 Using photo 1 as a guide, bend all four of the spacer bars with flat-nose pliers. Vary the bend points so that each earring has its own skyscraper profile. You might want to make some card-stock patterns of the spacer bar to try the bends on it first. The angles of the bends in the spacer bars don't have to match, but the bent bars must have the same lengths.

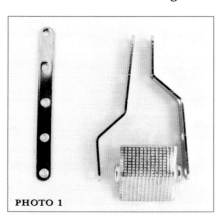

PHOTO 1

PHOTO 2

2 Put a bar, a square bead, and a second bar onto a micro-bolt. Twist the nut into place until it's almost touching the bar. Apply a drop of cement in the space between the nut and the bar; then twist the nut on so it's snug (photo 2). Trim the end of the bolt with heavy-duty wire cutters, and smooth the cut end with a nail file.

PHOTO 3

3 Open a jump ring and attach one of the spacer bars. Add a spacer disc bead and then the other bar (photo 3). Before closing the ring, attach an ear wire (photo 4).

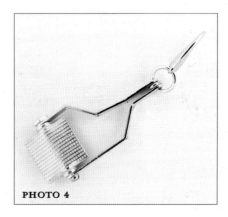

PHOTO 4

Repeat steps 2 and 3 to complete the second earring.

ring around the sparkle

The recessed area inside a wide hoop earring
is the perfect seat for a sparkly cup chain.

MATERIALS

2 brass hoop earrings
with a curved recess
facing the inside
circumference
Teal green nail polish
Teal crystal cup chain
Clear, multipurpose
jeweler's cement
with a precision
applicator tip

TOOLS

Wire cutters
Clothespins

DIMENSIONS

1¹³⁄₁₆ inches (4.6 cm)
in diameter

procedure

1 Paint the inside rims of the hoops with the nail polish (photo 1). After allowing the polish to dry, apply two or three more coats of polish. You want a very smooth, lacquered finish. Set the hoops aside to dry (photo 1).

PHOTO 1

2 Starting with one end of the cup chain and working in 1-inch (2.5 cm) sections, adhere the cup chain to the inner rim of one of the hoops with the multipurpose cement. Use clothespins to hold the chain in place while the cement adheres (photo 2).

PHOTO 2

3 Continue working in small sections until all of the chain is in place. Trim the excess chain with wire cutters (photo 3).

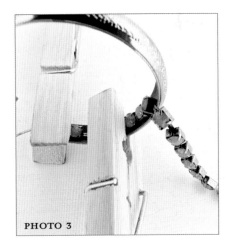

PHOTO 3

Repeat steps 2 and 3 to make the second earring.

square chic

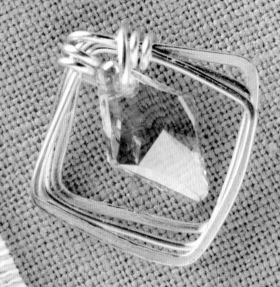

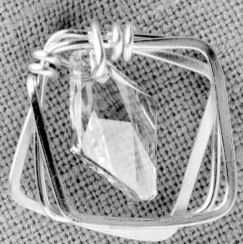

Simple-but-classic post earrings like these are easy to make with a jewelry jig tool. A few minutes, a couple of wraps, and you're good to go!

procedure

1 Make a 90° bend with the chain-nose pliers about ½ inch (1.3 cm) from the end of your wire (photo 1). This is the post for your earring.

3 Slide the wire shape off the mandrel and lay it on the edge of the steel block. Hammer the square shape with the flat face of your chasing hammer (photo 3).

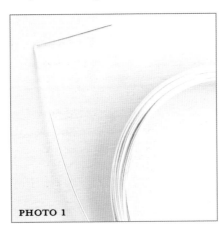

PHOTO 1

2 Secure the square mandrel to the jig, following the manufacturer's instructions. Position the bend in the wire at the corner of the square and wrap the wire once around the mandrel. The wrapped section will be shaped like a diamond (photo 2).

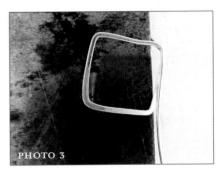

PHOTO 3

MATERIALS

Half-hard sterling wire, 20 gauge

2 crystal rhombus charms, 14 x 5 mm

2 acrylic or rubber earring backs

TOOLS

Wire cutters

Chain-nose pliers

Jewelry jig with a ⅞-inch (2.2 cm) square mandrel attachment

Sandpaper or cup burr

Steel block

Chasing hammer

DIMENSIONS

⅞ x ⅞ inches (2.2 cm)

VARIATION

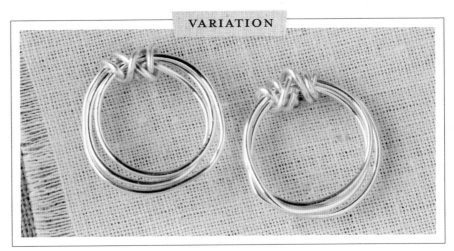

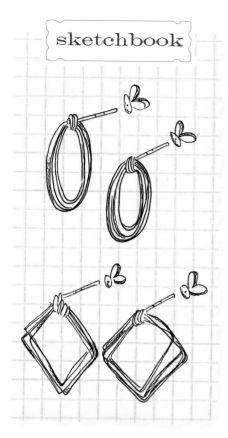

4 Position the wire back onto the square mandrel and make two more wraps (photo 4).

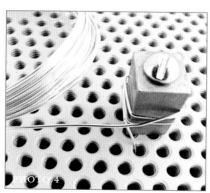

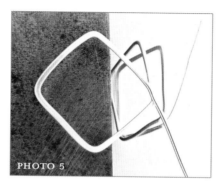

PHOTO 5

5 Fold the first two wraps away so that the third one can be laid down on the steel block (photo 5). Flatten it as you did in step 3. Realign the wire diamond shapes so they lie closely to each other.

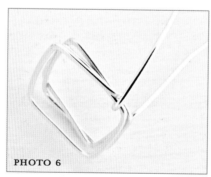

PHOTO 6

6 Trim the tail of the un-shaped wire to 4 inches (10.2 cm). Wrap this tail around all three diamonds, near the post, as shown in photo 6.

7 String a crystal charm onto the wire tail (photo 7); then wrap the trio of diamond-shaped wires around the other side of the post.

PHOTO 7

Trim the excess wire and tuck in the tails.

8 Trim the post section to an appropriate length—usually 9 to 10 mm works well. File the post's end with the sandpaper or cup burr to smooth it (photo 8). Finally, place an earring back over the post.

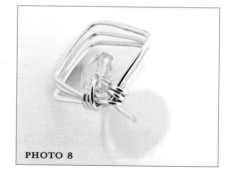

PHOTO 8

Repeat these steps to make the second earring.

around
the pond

Once upon a time, I lived in a little log cabin near a pond.
I would walk my dog, Rocker, around the pond and we would always
see green frogs on lily pads hanging out in the brown water.
That's what I think about when I look at these earrings.

procedure

1 Cut a 1½ inch (3.8 cm) piece of the brass wire, and make a teeny-tiny spiral at one end. (Use the very tip of your round-nose pliers, so it's not too big.) Coil the remainder of the short wire piece into a loose spiral (photo 1).

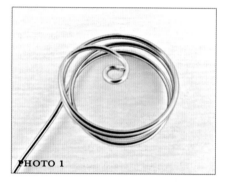

PHOTO 1

2 Nestle one of the large brown pearl beads into the coil you made in step 1. Position it so the wire spirals up and around its sides. String a balled head pin through the tiny wire spiral and through the pearl bead (photo 2).

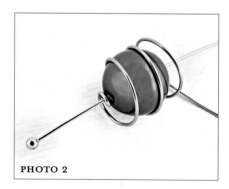

PHOTO 2

PHOTO 3

Adjust and trim the end of the spiraled wire, leaving enough tail to make another small loop at the end. Then trim the end of the balled head pin as necessary and make a simple loop there (photo 3).

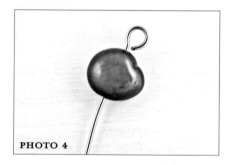

PHOTO 4

3 String a green pearl onto the piece of 24-gauge wire and finish the end with a simple loop (photo 4); finish the opposite end of the wire with a wrapped loop, but don't trim the wire yet.

Instead, twirl the tail around the bead, finishing with a wrap around the simple loop (photo 5). Trim the excess wire with the wire cutters.

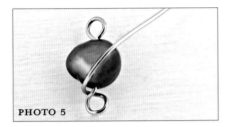

PHOTO 5

4 Open the simple loop in the large brown pearl and connect it to the green pearl bead link (photo 6).

PHOTO 6

5 Repeat the wrapping technique from step 3 for one of the smaller brown pearl beads. This time, slip the loop onto the green pearl bead link before wrapping the wire around the face of the brown pearl and its simple loop (photo 7).

PHOTO 7

PHOTO 8

6 Open the simple loop on the small brown pearl and connect the beaded dangle to the ear wire (photo 8).

Repeat these steps to make the second earring.

acknowledgments

To Lark Books and Sterling Publishing, thank you for keeping me around as one of your authors. I love being part of the Lark/Sterling family.

Thank you, Nathalie Mornu for moving this book through the acquisitions process and getting approval on it! I love working with you.

Kevin Kopp! Thanks over and over for all the hard work on this book. From edits to photo work, to just being nice, I can't thank you enough. I'm glad we got to work together.

Suzanne Tourtillot, thank you for mauling over the pages in this book to make sure every head pin, bead, and ear wire was used (and, more importantly, clearly explained how to be used)! I really loved working with you.

Pretty books happen because of you, Kathy Holmes! Your page layouts and ideas have inspired us to make things and continue our hobbies. That's important. THANK YOU!

Special thanks to Kay Holmes Stafford for the layout of this book. The pages look simply great!

Lynne Harty, your photos are always stunning. Thanks for fussing over the pieces to make them look perfect.

To those people that have worked on this book, that I've not interacted with or met, I know you're out there and this is probably my one chance to say thank you to YOU.

To my friends and fellow artists, you guys keep me going and I thank you over and over for that! Your check-ins, coffee meet ups, and visits—I really can't thank you enough.

Thank you over and over to Bead Trust, Craft Attitude, Tierra Cast, Alacarte Clasps, Vintaj, Ornamentea, Beadalon, Plaid Enterprises, Piddix Collage Sheets, Now That's A Jig, Jesse James Beads, Dakota Stones, Lilly Pilly, Garland Chain, and Swarovski Create Your Style for supporting *Earringology* by generously providing materials to create the projects in this book!

index